Danville, Virginia

AND THE COMING OF THE MODERN SOUTH

MICHAEL SWANSON

ISBN: 1449988059
ISBN-13: 9781449988050

TABLE OF CONTENTS

PREFACE

Looking back from the vantage point of today most people see the 1960s and the Civil Rights movement as being the period of critical change in the history of the South. These times brought a revolution in not only race relations and politics, but also in the economy of the South. However, the events of the 1960s had their origins in the twenty years preceding them. I hope this will become clear to you by the time you reach the end of this book.

Political alignments were much different after the Civil War than they are today. Today most people associate Republicans with a conservative small government political philosophy and aggressive foreign policy and Democrats with modern day liberalism. However, the Republican Party first took power in the White House under the leadership of Abraham Lincoln as a nationalist party that advocated using tariffs and taxes to encourage industry and eventually repudiated slavery, while the Democratic party opposed these measures and sought to defend slavery. After the Civil War the Democratic Party remained heavily influenced by Southern Democrats who fought to maintain a limited size of government and racial segregation through much of the twentieth century.

Contemporary Southerners called the era following the Civil War and Reconstruction the New South, a time in which the Democratic Party retook control of the states south of the Mason-Dixon line by defeating a political alliance of what they claimed were Northern carpetbaggers and black Republicans. The party then limited voting through the poll tax and created legal segregation while a new class of Southern elites jump-started the region's economy through investments in industry, particularly railroads and textiles. The political underpinnings of the New South lived on well into the 1960s, although some cracks in it began to emerge during the Presidency of Franklin Roosevelt..

This work is an attempt to examine some of these big themes in the history of the American South through a narrative history of Danville, Virginia. Events in Danville were key to the emergence of the New South Democrats in Virginia at the turn of twentieth century. Danville also became home to the largest textile plant in the country, making it a good place to look to understand the evolution of the Southern textile industry, how it impacted a community, and the people behind it. Despite the industry's reputation for poor working conditions and wages, the textile workers in Danville experienced a revolution in their living standards and social place in the 1940s, which became a precursor to changes that would occur throughout the entire South in the next thirty years.

This book begins with a short chapter on the fall of the Confederacy. In the final moments of the Civil War the Confederate government retreated from Richmond, Virginia, to Danville. The end of the war marked the end of slavery in the South. Southerners battled each other over the legacy of the war and what type of society they wanted to live in. In Virginia these political battles culminated in the Danville "riot" of 1883, which I detail in the second chapter of this book.

Danville became home to what would become the largest textile plant in the United States, Dan River Mills. I examine the rise of this company and the impact it had in Danville in the following three chapters of this book. The first of these chapters tells the story of the rise of this company and how it came to dominate the city's social and political structures. The second of these chapters narrates an important strike at Dan River Mills in 1930, while the last chapter of this series explains how World War II and Franklin Roosevelt's New Deal programs impacted the lives of the workers in Danville and transformed Danville's economy and politics. The last chapter in the book shows how Virginia's political leaders began to feel threatened by these changes and sought to keep their state fixed in history.

While much of Danville's past reflects events that took place in other Southern communities, I think a close study of the lives of several individuals in Danville helps one understand what it was like to live during these times. Thankfully there is a rich collection of doctoral dissertations, congressional hearings into the 1883 "race riot," biographies, diaries, interviews, and secondary works, that I have built on to write this book. In particular I found William Mainwaring's doctoral thesis *Community in Danville, Virginia, 1880-1963*, indispensable in the initial phases of my research, while Tim Minchin's *What Do We Need a Union For?* helped me to see how important some of the events in Danville were to understanding the overall history of textile unions in the South.

INTRODUCTION: On the Ashes of the Confederacy

April 2, 1865. For four years the Civil War had raged across America, with fierce fighting as far north as Gettysburg and as far west as New Mexico. Virginia, Kentucky, Tennessee, and the states along the Mississippi river from Missouri to Louisiana became famous for the battles that shaped the outcome of this epic struggle.

For the most part though, the major cities of the South had been untouched by war, but this drastically changed with the defeat of the Confederate army of the West at the Battle of Chattanooga. The Union armies, led by William Tecumseh Sherman, then had an opening into the very heartland of the Confederacy. Sherman marched his army into South Carolina and up toward North Carolina. However, the Confederate capital of Richmond, Virginia, only sixty miles from Washington, D.C., avoided capture.

In Virginia Confederate politicians, dignitaries, and their wives had left their plantations in the hands of overseers and watched the war rage around them from the safety of Richmond. Family and friends died in battle, other cities and states fell to the Union, but by and large the people of Richmond had avoided the horrible tragedies of the war. In fact, many of them lived in comfort. In one day that came to an end. April 2 fell on a Sunday and most of Richmond went to church just like they always did on any given Sunday.

A courier for the Confederate War Department, knowing he would find President Jefferson Davis in attendance at St. Paul's Episcopal Church, entered during the morning service. Spotting him sitting in the front pew, the courier handed him a telegram and slipped out of the building. Worshipers, sitting near their President, noticed a "sort of gray pallor" of color sweep over his face. The telegram, written by General Robert E. Lee, informed him that the lines protecting Petersburg and Richmond could no longer be defended. Nothing could now prevent the Union army from entering the city. Lee recommended to Davis that "all preparation be made for leaving Richmond tonight."[1]

With the warning of the note, Davis got up and left "with stern set lips and his usual quick military tread." He went to the War Office and met with his top military staff and cabinet. Together they gathered the most important government documents needed to keep the government functioning and fled south by train. They planned to take the Confederate Capital with them.

Retreating Confederate troops torched warehouses full of supplies. Fires broke out throughout Richmond. By the time the fires burnt out almost three-fourths of the city lay smoldering. Looters took whatever they could before the fires got to it.[2]

Riding the rails, Jefferson Davis and his cohorts were determined not to let the loss of Richmond mean the end of the Southern government. John Wise, a young Confederate Lieutenant, watched the trains pass him by. "A government on wheels…it was the marvelous and incongruous debris of the wreck of the Confederate capital," he recalled. One car housed $528,000 in gold and Mexican silver, protected by a contingent of sixty men. "But," Wise said, "among the last in the long procession were trains bearing indiscriminate cargoes of men and things. In one car was a cage with an African parrot and a box of tame squirrels, and a hunchback! Everybody, not excepting the parrot, was wrought up to a pitch of intense excitement."[3]

---

1 Shelby Foote, *The Civil War a Narrative: Red River to Appomattox* (New York: Vintage, 1974), p.885; John Brubaker III, *The Last Capital* (Danville, Virginia: McCain Printing, 1979), p.4.

2 Foote, pp.885-889; Virginius Dabney, *Virginia* (Charlottesville: University Press of Virginia, 1971), p.350.

3 Brubaker, p.7; Foote, p.890.

The train's destination, Danville, Virginia, a small town popu-
lated with four thousand people, sat near the North Carolina
border in Pittsylvania County. Built on the banks of the Dan River,
Danville had served as the central market for regional Piedmont
tobacco planters and as home to several tobacco factories. The
Confederate army converted some of the tobacco warehouses
into supply depots, two as hospitals and six as prisons for Union
troops captured in battle.[4]

Jefferson Davis and General Lee made a deliberate decision
to move the Southern government to Danville. The town lay
between the two main remaining Confederate armies of Lee in
Virginia and Joseph Johnston in North Carolina. They planned for
Lee and Johnston to meet at Danville and then attack the Union
army with their combined forces. Davis had also feared that moving the capital out of Virginia would further weaken the government politically. The best place to retreat seemed to be Danville.[5]

Once Davis arrived in Danville he received a warm reception from the city's leaders, who had decided to use the home
of William T. Sutherlin as a temporary capital for Davis. Sutherlin
built a fortune as a planter, dealer, and manufacturer of tobacco
and became one of the most prominent tobacco merchants in
Virginia. So large were his operations that Sutherlin possessed
the second-largest tobacco factory in the state, using the labor of
forty slaves he owned and forty others that he hired from other
slaveholders.[6]

While Sutherlin owned slaves, he did not see himself as an
aristocrat, like many other Southern plantation owners did. He
believed that society was comprised of classes, "but of the individuals that comprise them," he wrote, "many are constantly
passing from one another as changes occur in their circumstances
and fortunes…Indeed there are few of our prominent men who if

---

4 Brubaker, pp.14-17.
5 Ibid., p.5.
6 Barbara Bennett, *William T. Sutherlin and the Danville Tobacco Industry* (M.A.: University
   of North Carolina at Greensboro, 1974), p.8.

they undertook to trace their genealogy, would not soon run into the mud; while there are many imbeciles now in the mire who can easily trace their ancestry back to aristocracy." Like other famous Virginians who came before him, such as Thomas Jefferson, Sutherlin argued that those of wealth and privilege owed service to their communities and country and those of lesser ability should follow them for guidance.[7]

He lived those words as best he could. After rising to prominence in business, Sutherlin rose in social prestige and power. He served on the board of two of Danville's banks, cofounded the first local insurance agency, and acted as a leading Freemason. Freemasonry became so important to him that he gave huge sums of money to build a new three-story Masonic Lodge that dwarfed the town's rustic skyline. He eventually became mayor of Danville, holding office for six years, from 1855 to 1861.[8]

When Southern states began talking of secession in 1861, Sutherlin served as one of two delegates from Pittsylvania County for Virginia's secession convention. Sutherlin, as well as many in Danville and the county were lukewarm about secession, and local politicians often criticized both Northern abolitionists and South Carolina secessionists. In letters to friends, Sutherlin expressed more fears about war levies than abolitionism. Other local businessmen also worried that high taxes would be needed to pay for a Southern war effort. Pittsylvania County's other delegate joined Sutherlin in voting against secession.

However, once the Union bombarded Fort Sumter, Danville followed the rest of Virginia in support of the Southern cause. Although much of Virginia lay devastated by war, Danville, untouched by battle, benefited from the conflict. Sutherlin, given the rank of Major, served as commander of Danville's Confederate supply operations. This allowed him to convince the Confederate government to extend the Richmond-Danville rail line to

---

7 Frederick Siegel, *The Roots of Southern Distinctiveness: Tobacco and Society in Danville Virginia* (Chapel Hill: University of North Carolina Press, 1987), p.144.
8 Ibid., p.141.

Greensboro, North Carolina, an act that greatly increased rail traffic through the city and strengthened its economic vitality.[9]

Now Sutherlin opened his home up to the fleeing government and President Jefferson Davis. His large house, with stucco walls and a square cupola, served as the last Confederate Capitol for a week. Cut off from General Lee and his Army and with only sporadic updates on the war, Jefferson Davis spent most of his stay holding periodic cabinet meetings during the day and dining with Sutherlin in the evening.

Davis held a lengthy cabinet meeting inside of the mansion on its first day as the Confederate Capitol on April 4, 1865. Afterward, he went into Sutherlin's library and penned an upbeat proclamation designed to reassure the rest of the South that the fall of Richmond did not mean the end of the Confederacy. Instead, he argued that it provided a new opportunity in the war; by freeing up Lee's army from a need to protect the city it would allow him to launch a new attack on the Union army. "We have now entered upon a new phase of a struggle, the memory of which is to endure for all ages, and to shed even-increasing luster upon our country," he wrote. The document turned out to be the President's first official act in Danville and his last as President of the Confederacy.[10]

Cut off from outside news, Davis spent most of the week wondering when Lee would bring his army to Danville. With little information to go by, he held short cabinet meetings. Navy Secretary Stephen Mallory remembered, "to a few, a very few, they were days of hope; to the many they were days of despondency, if not despair, and to all days of intense anxiety." Finally, on April 8, news came when Lieutenant John Wise, a courier sent by Lee, rode his horse to the Sutherlin mansion.[11]

Wise, ushered into a dining room where Davis and a few other cabinet members were present, informed them that Lee's army had been smashed at Sayler's Creek and surrender remained the

9 Ibid., p.154.
10 Brubaker, pp.28-29.
11 Ibid., p.47.

General's only option. After the cabinet meeting ended, Wise ate a needed meal in the dining room and then joined Davis in the parlor. After more discussion on the condition of Lee's army, Davis sat silently "peering into the gloom outside," Wise recalled.[12]

The next day Lee surrendered his army to General Ulysses Grant at Appomattox. Davis, determined to carry on the war, put his government on board the Presidential train once again and fled farther South to Greensboro, North Carolina. Later in the afternoon a Confederate cavalry regiment entered Danville with orders to destroy the railway bridge that crossed the Dan River and to burn down all of the military warehouses to slow down the Union army.

Colonel Robert Withers, a personal friend of Sutherlin and commander of the local Danville military post, tried to discourage the cavalry from carrying out their orders. Withers ordered his men to guard the bridge and resist with violence if necessary. Unwilling to fight one last purposeless battle, the cavalry turned away.[13]

The war came to an end just as quietly. When Davis arrived in Greensboro, no one stood by the train to greet him. Fearing reprisals from the advancing Union army for any courtesy extended to Davis, Greensboro's leading citizens decided to simply ignore him. After years of war, pragmatism had come to replace the fighting spirit of the Piedmont.[14]

Back in Danville, rumors that food supplies packed the city's warehouses sparked riots among thousands of malnourished Confederate troops still left in the city. Outnumbered by the rioters Colonel Withers and his militia failed to contain the mob. Chaos ruled. Professor Charles Morris of Randolph-Macon College recalled seeing "the throwing open of the large stores collected here to the heterogeneous assemblage of soldiers, citizens, refugees, stragglers, camp-followers, and Negroes."[15]

---

12 Ibid., p.49.
13 Siegel, pp.158-159.
14 Foote, p.965.
15 Edward Pollock, *Sketch Book of Danville*, reprint edition (Danville: McCain Printing Company, 1993), p.60.

When Federal troops arrived in town, they were greeted with cordiality. City leaders were relieved as the Union troops restored order. General Wright, the Union commander, pitched his tent next to the Sutherlin mansion. Sutherlin met the general and extended his friendship. Colonel Withers went so far as to welcome Union officers to his house for evening meals with a view of the final Capitol of the Confederacy outside of their window. In Danville the war ended with handshakes, but no one knew what would come tomorrow.[16]

The Civil War laid Virginia to waste. The state suffered more devastation than any other state in the Confederacy. Thousands of Virginians died in battle. Richmond lay in ruins. So did fields, roads, and crops across the countryside. The tobacco industry, which Danville relied upon, faced an uneasy future. Thanks to the war, the soil had been neglected, property values plummeted, credit became nonexistent, and slavery had been eliminated.

All life in the Southern states had centered on slavery. Its end meant the collapse of a political and legal system that had governed Virginia's social relations and economic system for decades. William Sutherlin and other Southern landowners faced a giant void in front of them. What would it mean for the future now that the Confederacy was gone and the Union army occupied the South?

The Federal government would soon create a new state government. How would it bring peace when so much confusion seemed to lie ahead? Would the newly freed slaves agitate to employ the powers of the new government against the interests of the old slave owners? Would the end of the Civil War mean only the beginning of a new war of Virginians against Virginians? How could a new state gain the respect and obedience of a society whose interests were so divided?

---

16 Siegel, p. 159.

CHAPTER ONE: Colonel Cabell's Coup: *The Danville Riot*

Confederate soldiers came home from the war to start a new life under their victors' terms. Initially they thought about the meaning of what they had gone through, because they had to come to grips with the past before facing the future. John Mosby, a guerrilla cavalry leader who raided Union forces and supplies behind enemy lines, capturing one Union general and at times hanging prisoners, said, "I have never apologized for anything I did during or since the war... It was our country and we fought for it and we did not care whether it was right or wrong.... I committed treason and am proud of it."[17]

Others felt differently. Thomas Settle, who fought for the Confederacy for one year, thought that "the war was commenced to perpetuate slavery. It went the other way, contrary to all the leaders of the rebellion. Therefore, slavery is forever dead. This has been the work of God, and I can say that it is for the best."[18]

Days after the Confederate surrender, General James Longstreet reunited with Robert E. Lee in Lynchburg, Virginia. Longstreet would eventually move to New Orleans and start over again as a successful businessman. Generals Beauregard, Hood, Magruder, and Wilcox also made the city their home. Longstreet told his Southern listeners, "We are a conquered people" who

---

17 David Blight, *Race and Reunion: The Civil War in American Memory* (Massachusetts: Kelknap Press, 2001), pp.297-298.
18 Ibid., p.48.

have to face this fact and "accept the terms that are now offered by the conquerors."[19]

Not every Confederate accepted defeat. General Jubal Early fled to Mexico and vowed to never return to Virginia as long as the Stars and Stripes flew over it. Due to poverty he did, in fact, return to his home in Lynchburg in 1869 and became an unreconstructed rebel who would never give in.[20]

Although Confederates were divided over what to make of the peace, Southerners had never been wholly united. Before the war began many of them, such as William Sutherlin, opposed leaving the Union, although once it began they supported the war effort. Pockets of ardent opposition continued to exist throughout the war in Virginia's southwest mountains and Shenandoah Valley where few slaves were owned. These union loyalists, along with freed slaves, small farmers, and transplanted Northerners became core supporters of the Republican Party after the Civil War. Their opponents tended to be Confederate veterans, wealthy landowners, and bankers who eventually gravitated to the Democratic Party.

Moderate political leaders in Virginia tried to operate from the middle of these groups in the two decades following the Civil War in order to steer the ship of state on a course that would benefit most of its passengers. Their efforts ended in failure when a conservative faction in Virginia feared that they would be voted out of existence. In 1883, they overthrew the town government of Danville, Virginia, and through intimidation and terror took over the governor's mansion and the General Assembly.

The Rise of General William Mahone

During these times, General William Mahone became one of the most loved and despised people in Virginia. Mahone served under General Robert E. Lee and became a war hero at the battle of the

---

19 Jeffry Wert, *General James Longstreet: The Confederacy's Most Controversial Soldier* (New York: Simon and Schuster, 1993), pp.409-10.
20 Blight, p.78.

crater in Petersburg, Virginia. Scrawny, weighing only a hundred pounds and standing five feet five, at first glance he didn't look like a hero. His fingers were tapered like a woman's and his feet were small and narrow. Despite delivering his orders with a squeaky voice, one of his subordinates called him "the biggest little man God almighty ever made."

Mahone carried a special cage of chickens with him on his military campaigns to cure a score of digestive problems. He also occasionally dabbled in hard liquor, a habit he may have picked up as a child when he grew up around a family owned pub. After leaving home, Mahone earned an engineering degree at the Virginia Military Institute. He then went into the railroad business and by 1861 had risen to become the president, chief engineer, and superintendent of the Norfolk and Petersburg Railroad, amassing a fortune in the process.

Once the Confederacy surrendered, Mahone returned to the railroad business with the goal of consolidating several railroad lines that had been built before the war. Dozens of small railroads existed throughout the state and he planned to combine some of them in order to create one line that would stretch across Virginia and into Tennessee by linking the Norfolk, Petersburg, and Lynchburg lines into one big company. In these efforts he found himself opposed by the Baltimore and Ohio Railroad, which wanted to build a route of its own in Virginia.

Mahone and the B&O battled against each other to get the cooperation of the state government for their plans. Virginia had helped build many of the lines before the Civil War and owned about half of the stock in all of the state's railroads, so its approval was critical. Governor Francis Pierpont, who had been appointed provisional governor of Virginia by the federal government, believed that Mahone's plan would be advantageous to his state.[21]

---

21 Virginius Dabney, *Virginia, The New Dominion: A History from 1607 to the Present* (Charlottesville: University of Virginia Press, 1971), pp. 374-375; Jack Maddex, Jr., *The Virginia Conservatives* (Chapel Hill: University of North Carolina Press, 1970), pp. 143-150.

The B&O sent lobbyists and agents to the Virginia Assembly to convince lawmakers to support their efforts to build a line from Harper's Ferry, through the Shenandoah Valley, and into Tennessee, which would thwart Mahone's plans and, in the belief of Governor Pierpont, would cause economic harm to the state. Mahone needed to stop them by lobbying the politicians himself. "You had better spend," the governor wrote, "ten thousand dollars than let this legislature fail...commerce and money have no conscience when great commercial interests are to be obtained. Richmond, Norfolk, and Petersburg, and even Lynchburg are ruined commercially if you don't succeed... you must get your men."

Another supporter informed Mahone that in the General Assembly "there are two men who can be purchased at $500 each...if you want me, telegraph and I will come. Consolidation must be accomplished without regard to cost. Without it we die with dry rot." Mahone took out all of the stops, dispensing not only money, but railroad passes and booze to win over the legislators.[22]

They granted him his wish, passing legislation that allowed him to buy up the lines he desired and combine them into a new company, the Atlantic, Mississippi, and Ohio. The railroads were in poor condition, with sections of track left destroyed by the war. Mahone quickly spent money to fix them. The general improved most of the lines, but didn't have the funds to repair the section west of Lynchburg and wasn't able to combine all of them together. Mahone couldn't completely fend off the B&O, and within a few years he found the political terrain in Richmond had shifted. He would have to use his influence to win new friends and make new alliances.[23]

Mahone the Politician

After the Confederacy surrendered, the U.S. Congress, dominated by the Republican Party, passed the thirteenth amendment to the

---

22 Nelson Blake, *William Mahone of Virginia: Soldier and Political Insurgent* (Alabama: University of Alabama Press, 1966), pp.82-83).

23 Maddex, pp.152-153.

Constitution, which freed the slaves. They followed that act with the fourteenth amendment, granting citizenship to former slaves and disqualifying Confederate officeholders from serving in government. A year later Congress passed the Reconstruction Act, which placed all of the Southern states under military occupation until they created new state constitutions.

Some entrusted with the role of "occupier" antagonized Virginia's white conservatives. Judge John Underwood became the most infamous of these men. A native of New York, Underwood had moved to Virginia and operated a dairy farm before the Civil War. He became a fierce opponent of slavery, and, chased out by death threats, fled the state. Once the war ended, the Federal government appointed him as Virginia's district judge, a position he used to prosecute Jefferson Davis for treason.

With a snide manner, Underwood delivered his charges. He claimed that the Confederate army had "burned down towns and cities with a barbarity unknown to Christian countries, scattered yellow fever and smallpox among the poor and helpless," and, referring to Abraham Lincoln, "finally struck down one of earth's noblest martyrs to freedom and humanity." The judge argued that Jefferson Davis had brought so much "licentiousness" to Richmond that "probably a majority of the births were illegitimate." Newspapers across the state howled with ringing denunciations of Underwood. Davis never went to trial. After posting bond, his case got shelved after Republican politicians in Washington decided that it would only purposelessly antagonize the South.

Although the prosecution of Davis ended, Judge Underwood didn't disappear from the news. Within months he chaired Virginia's Constitutional Convention, much to the chagrin of conservatives across the state, who were prevented from voting because they had supported the Confederacy. Seventy-two of the delegates were Republicans, twenty-five of whom were black, while only thirty-three delegates were white conservatives. The Richmond newspapers published vicious attacks against the convention and its proceedings, calling it the "Mongrel Convention," the "Convention of Kangaroos," the "Black Crook Convention," and the "Bones and Banjo Convention."[24]

When the draft for the new constitution was finished, it gave Virginia its first educational system, made the tax system more equitable, granted universal male suffrage, forbid discrimination in jury selection, and created a township system of local government. The constitution also made it illegal for Confederate veterans to vote.

The constitution, brought up as a referendum for the voters, guaranteed factionalism. Some Republicans wanted people they saw as traitors removed from public life; while conservatives feared that it would put radical Republicans and blacks in a situation in which they would rule over them with impunity. Although it never was a large force in Virginia, the Klu Klux Klan found itself with a bounty of new recruits and attempted to intimidate voters and Republicans. One prominent Republican received a letter promising that he would die on sunset the day before the election.[25]

Pittsylvania County, the home of Danville, became the biggest center of electoral conflict in the state. Landowners in the county threatened to evict sharecroppers from their land if they voted for the constitution. One Federal official said that he received a "great many complaints...of assaults on the freedpeople by the whites." In a "remote part of the county" the freed slaves "are taken out of their houses at night by men armed and disguised who beat them with sticks." Their attackers "take their guns, knives and any weapon they may find," and "in several cases have demanded money," he wrote. The family of Wesley Edward had been singled out. His attackers "threatened the life of his wife who was sick in bed and then ravished his daughter." Some "colored men have been compelled to leave their cabins and sleep in the woods," he reported.[26]

---

24 Dabney, pp.363-367.
25 Richard Lowe, *Republicans and Reconstruction in Virginia* 1856-1870, (Charlottesville: The University of Virginia, 1991), pp.125, 141-145.
26 Jeffrey Kerr-Ritchie, *Freedpeople in the Tobacco South: Virginia,* 1860-1900 (Chapel Hill: University of North Carolina Press), pp.87-88.

Although many conservatives said they would rather die than see the new constitution passed, several prominent Virginian leaders came to the conclusion that they would have to accept the reality of Federal occupation and make the best of it. They nominated a committee of nine men, which included William Mahone, William Sutherlin, and several Republican moderates, to try to come up with a compromise. The men traveled to Washington, D.C., and lobbied to get the constitutional clauses which would disenfranchise former Confederate supporters to be voted on separately from the rest of the constitution.[27]

Their efforts proved successful and the constitution eventually passed without the disenfranchising clauses. Also on the ballot was the question of who was to be the next governor. With thousands of former slaves now voting for the first time, it became clear that the Republican Party's candidate would be sworn in to the governor's mansion. The only possible opposition to the Republicans could have come from the Conservative Party, but they decided not to field a candidate. Nevertheless, the race was not a one-man affair.[28]

Two men ran to be nominated as the Republicans' choice for governor: Union General H. Wells and Gilbert Walker. Wells, a supporter of the disenfranchising clauses, had been the Federal army's provisional occupation governor and was popular with radical Republicans and freedmen. Walker, a native New Yorker who moved to Norfolk after the Union occupied it, served on the committee of nine and received the backing of moderate Republicans and conservatives.[29]

Mahone decided to do all he could to support Walker's candidacy behind the scenes, using his money and influence to get Dr. J. D. Harris, a black physician, chosen as Wells's running mate for lieutenant governor. Thinking that no white Virginian

---

27 Barbara Bennett, *William T. Sutherlin and the Danville Tobacco Industry* (M.A. Thesis: University of North Carolina at Greensboro, 1974), p.9.

28 Lowe, p. 171.

29 Dabney, pp.370-371.

would vote for a black man, Mahone had calculated that this would split Wells's votes up along racial lines. The general then sent bags of cash to Walker, gave him free railroad passes to hand out to potential voters, and even helped him write his speeches.[30]

On Election Day, July 6, 1869, Gilbert Walker defeated former Union General H. H. Wells by 199,000 to 101,000 votes. With the new state constitution passed, the Federal troops left Virginia and ended their occupation. Conservative and moderate Virginians rejoiced. Walker appeared on a balcony and congratulated Virginia on her deliverance from "vampires and harpies." Bonfires were lighted below and the sound of "Dixie" could be heard in the air as the Yankee Walker liberated Virginia.[31]

Mahone's honeymoon with Walker did not last for long. He expected Walker to be favorable to his railroad schemes. The governor had been a director of the Norfolk and Petersburg railroads and a leading banker, a fact that could have made it possible for Walker to give Mahone's railroads financial backing. Instead, Walker opened up the 1869 Virginia Assembly and announced his decision to sell off Virginia's ownership in the state's railroads to Mahone's competitors. He called his plan "free railroads." Mahone called it a betrayal.

The governor's brother, James Walker, descended on the state capitol as a lobbyist for the Pennsylvania Railroad Company. Owned by Thomas Scott, the Penn was the largest railroad in the world at the time. Inside the governor's mansion the two brothers devised a plan to sell the state's interests in the Richmond and Danville Railroad to Scott's company. In return, Scott gave James Walker two thousand shares of Pennsylvania stock. The state legislators were showered with lavish entertainment and money in return for looking the other way.[32]

---

30 Lowe, p. 175.
31 Dabney, pp. 372-373.
32 Blake, pp. 105, 154.

The governor didn't stop there. Northern companies, with the blessings of gubernatorial sanction, continued to buy up the most desirable rail lines in the state. The Baltimore and Ohio bought the Orange and Alexandria Railroad, while the Southern Railway Security Company, a front for Thomas Scott, bought control of the Richmond and Petersburg shares. Mahone had offered $200 a share for the line, but the governor decided to sell it to Scott for $150. The state lost over ten million dollars on its antebellum investments in the fire sale of its railroad interests.[33]

Decrying the rampant corruption, some newspaper commentators called the General Assembly "Virginia's worst legislature." The public agreed and reelected only twenty-six out of one hundred thirty-two members of the House of Delegates in the next election. "Free railroads" were not the only issue that drew the voter's ire.

The antebellum and Civil War Virginia state government had amassed an enormous public debt to the tune of forty-five million dollars, most of it owed to bondholders in Richmond and outside of the state who were receiving 6 percent interest. Governor Walker passed the Funding Act to pay off the debt. However, the sums required under this plan were so huge that the state didn't have sufficient funds to meet its expenses. Public services deteriorated rapidly, the school system fell apart, and taxes were raised.

Many Virginians didn't like watching their taxes go up while their schools closed their doors. The same regions of the state that were most opposed to the Confederacy were also most opposed to paying off the state debt. These included the western parts of the state and the Shenandoah Valley. They were also the most in need of assistance for small farmers. Freed blacks, in turn, did not believe that they should be forced to pay debts incurred by the Confederate state government before or during the Civil War. Those most supportive of the Funding Act included lawyers, plantation owners, and bankers. They considered it an

---

33 Maddex, pp. 154-155.

issue of "honor" to pay off the debt. Not coincidently, though, these were the groups in Virginia who owned portions of the debt themselves.

William Mahone entered the fray. Behind the scenes he worked to form a political alliance to oppose full payment of the state debts. At first he acted inside the Conservative Party, but after two Conservative governors occupied the capitol and supported debt payment, he decided to break away and form his own party, the Readjuster Party, bringing over several Conservative leaders with him.

Mahone and his cohorts worked to elect as many of their people as possible into the General Assembly. Their message spread like wildfire during the 1879 election season. White small farmers and mountain folk took up the Readjuster banner while freedmen, who had been Republicans, also became strong Readjuster supporters. For their black supporters, Mahone's party promised to create schools and a mental institution. He also promised to abolish the whipping post, a relic from the days of slavery. On Election Day his Readjusters won eighty-two thousand votes while the Conservatives garnered sixty-one thousand. Readjusters took fifty-six out of one hundred of the seats in the House of Delegates and twenty-four out of forty of the Senate seats. The only obstacle to their domination of Virginia politics was the governor's office, which still remained in Conservative hands.[34]

Despite their smashing victories, the Readjusters had a difficult time getting their legislative agenda passed over the governor's repeated veto, a problem that they decided to remedy in the 1881 gubernatorial race. In that race they ran William Cameron of Petersburg against John W. Daniel of Lynchburg, a strong proponent of debt payment. The two candidates debated across the state and after the election Cameron packed his bags for Richmond. More Readjusters followed his coattails and took seats in the assembly, including fourteen black candidates.

---

34 Dabney, pp. 376-384; John Melzer, *The Danville Riot, November 3, 1883* (M.A. Thesis: University of Virginia, 1963), pp. 12-13.

With the Readjusters in control of both houses of the General Assembly and the governor's office, they quickly enacted their agenda. They scaled back payments for the state debt, lowered taxes, abolished poll taxes, increased education funding by 50 percent, and founded a college for blacks in Petersburg. They kept their campaign promises, something that doesn't always happen in politics, and an act that made their popularity grow.

Mahone himself was appointed a seat in the United States Senate by the General Assembly. When Mahone joined the Senate, he found the chamber evenly divided between Republicans and Democrats. He broke ranks with the Democratic South and sided his Readjuster Party with the Republicans. In turn, he was given committee seats in the Senate, but was branded a "traitor to his state, his election, and his party," by Virginia Conservatives. Beaten by Readjuster victories and Mahone's popularity, the Conservatives believed they finally an issue to use against him.[35]

In the spring of 1883, John W. Daniel sent out telegrams and letters to Conservative leaders throughout the state telling them to meet in Lynchburg, Virginia, for their party's July convention. They came in droves for what would be their party's most important meeting. It had become clear that the debt issue had made it unpopular throughout the state and in order to attract more voters the party planned to completely reinvent itself.

Their first order of business was to change the party's name from "Conservative" to "Democrat." They also dropped the unpopular debt issue. The Richmond delegation wanted to put the issue of race into the platform, but the convention did not formally write it in, although the delegates agreed that they would unofficially make it the top issue of the campaign. Instead of losing on the debt issue, they would try to win by making an issue out of who was a real Southerner. That meant seeking white supremacist votes by demonizing Mahone as a supporter of Republicans and blacks. John Daniel put it best. When people would be asked

---

35 Dabney, p. 386, Melzer, pp. 13-14, William Tate, Jr., *The Danville Riot of 1883, Its Effects on Politics in Virginia* (M.A. Thesis: University of Richmond, 1968), p. 38.

which party they support they should say, "I am a Democrat because I am a white man and a Virginian."

John Barbour, the head of the Orange and Alexandria Railroad took up the post of chairman of the State Democratic Party. He organized the party in a military fashion, dividing up every ward into companies of fifty voters who were each assigned a "captain." In each company five "chiefs" were each responsible for making sure that ten voters went to the polls on Election Day. Barbour also dispatched, to each county, speakers, who whipped up support for the party by attacking Mahone as a tyrant and ally of Republicans and blacks.

Democrats spread their message through circulars and newspapers. In Carroll County they distributed a pamphlet that warned white voters not to vote for the Readjusters, because a vote for them meant voting "for mixed schools now and mixed marriages in the future." It also meant taking up "the African side in the Cameron side on your own race" and endorsing "Mahone's treason." The *Danville Times* noted:

> It will not be long before you will see Coalitionists advocating the repeal of the law forbidding the intermarriage of the two races...If you want to protect your wives and daughters and keep off bloodshed you must stand up like men for your race and civilization. Everything will look like Africa. A black will wait on ladies at different post-offices. A black boy will search the records for you in the clerk's office. Your bench of magistrates will be a half and half. Your Commonwealth's attorney may be a Negro, and a Negro will surely visit your house collecting taxes.[36]

The Danville Circular

As the Election Day of 1883 drew near, racial tensions boiled over in Danville, Virginia. Out of fifteen thousand people in the town and

---

36 Tate, pp. 41-49; Melzer, p.26; Senate of the United States Investigation of Danville Riot, Fourth Congress, *Alleged Outrages in Virginia Report No. 579*, May 27, 1884, p.4

the surrounding area more than half were black, a fact that made black voters play a large role in local politics. Two political parties were active in the town: the Democrats and the Coalitionists, an alliance of Readjusters and Republicans. Colonel George S. Cabell, a Confederate veteran, chaired the local Democratic Party while J. B. Raulston and Squire Taliaferro led the Coalitionists. The Democrats elected their candidates to the clerk of court, commonwealth's attorney, city treasurer, and magistrate, while the coalitionists took half of the city council seats and a Coalitionist served as chief of police. The commissioner of revenue and mayor, J. H. Johnston, were both Independents. Out of forty-four elected officials six were independents and eighteen were Coalitionists, leaving Democrats in the minority. Nine of the Coalitionists were black and so were four of the policemen.[37]

Democrats detested the presence of blacks in elected office. Some of the more rabid Democrats could not stand to see blacks and whites together in public. W. P. Robinson, a former city magistrate experienced this for himself when he accompanied a black laborer to the outskirts of town. As the two entered the town they parted and went their separate ways. Robinson walked past a man who had seen the two of them together. Then he heard a gun go off. He said:

> Well, I don't know whether he shot at me or not. I never could hear a pistol pass anyhow, I am a little deaf but that sort of thing made me feel in danger and I walked rapidly. I think he may have shot at me. I know how times were, and I met right opposite Pete Gould's house, a white man there, and I got within fifty feet of his back door and I heard someone say, 'O, God damn you.' I turned to look and saw the man take aim at me and fire. I drew a pistol and ran after him and he ran. He was at the top of the hill and he fired as he ran.[38]

---

37 U.S. Senate, p. 455; Tate, pp. 52-56.
38 Testimony of W. P. Robinson, U.S. Senate.

Similar incidents occurred as Election Day approached. While walking on the sidewalk Mrs. Cobb, a white woman, found her path blocked by a black woman who exclaimed, "Next time I meet you, get out of the way, and save the trouble of being knocked off!"

The mayor, J. H. Johnston, received enough complaints about people's behavior that he issued a public statement in response: "I hereby invite and request every citizen, white and colored, who feels himself aggrieved by the conduct of any official...to present their complaints to me at my office in a formal and definite manner, together with the evidence to sustain their charges; will be dealt with to the full extent of the law in each such case," it read.

Johnston's offer had no impact. All of the complaints he received were investigated, but evidence was too vague and insufficient to cause action to be taken. The perpetrators always remained unidentified. By August 1883, everyone in Virginia found out about the situation in Danville from the state's leading newspapers as they reported on a murder and lynching attempt in the town.[39]

After delivering a wagon full of produce, William Shepherd and his son left Danville. When they were only a few miles from the town three black men approached them and asked them for a ride. Shepherd refused. One of the men responded by drawing a pistol and shooting him in the head and in the stomach. Two other black men heard the shooting and rode up to the wagon to help Shepherd. As soon as the three hoodlums saw the other two men coming they fled the scene in panic. But the friendly men were too late. They found Shepherd dead and took his son back to Danville.

Once the police found out what happened, they immediately rounded up a group of blacks that they thought looked suspicious. The boy identified three of them. Although one of the men had a pistol, all three claimed innocence. The authorities planned to

---

39 Tate, pp.56-57.

take the prisoners to Chatham, the county seat, for a trial. After a train departed Chatham for Danville to get them, Mayor Johnston received a tip that a mob had plans to hold up the train, take the suspects off, and then lynch them after it left the town.

The train made it five miles to Danville. At that point around 150 masked men surrounded it and forced the conductor to let them check the cars. Once they found that the prisoners were not aboard, they let the train go and walked toward Danville. The conductor telegraphed Johnston and warned him that they were going to try to break into the jail. The mayor promptly ordered the police and the militia to surround it.

The mob reached Danville's city limits and stopped. Informed that the jail was under guard, they decided not to try to take it by storm, but to trickle into town in groups of five or six men at a time. They waited until dawn and made their move. The mob waited all day, but, under the protection of the local militia, the Danville Grays, the prisoners were put on the train and transferred to Lynchburg, Virginia. After a few days, things quieted down and the prisoners were taken to Chatham where they were tried, found guilty, and hanged.

The closer the 1883 election came the more Democrats in Danville began to draw attention to the race issue, just like their statewide counterparts were doing. The Third Ward Club, a local Democratic group led by Colonel George Cabell, tried to force people to choose sides. In October he announced a boycott of local black businesses, targeting grocers, barbers, and butchers. Danville's Democrats wrote complaints against blacks, which were printed throughout the state. One Danville Democrat wrote a Lynchburg newspaper: "White women are rudely shoved off the pavement by dirty buck Negroes and encouraged to do it by the truculent Negro policemen appointed by the Mahone ring."[40]

Rumors spread in town that any black person who tried to vote would be shot. A prominent white businessman stopped a

---

40 Melzer, pp. 27-29; Tate, p. 59.

black man he knew and told him, "I'm a friend of yours and I want to tell you not to be on the street. If you will vote go to the poll early and vote and then go to the country. Go if you have an excuse to go. I don't want you to be on the street on the day of the election. If you are, you'll be killed."

Squire Taliaferro received a similar warning when he went to buy some meat from a white butcher. "We're going to carry this town at all hazards!" the man told him. After Taliaferro asked how the Democrats would do that if they didn't have the votes, the butcher replied, "We're going to carry it, votes or no votes, with double-barrel shotguns, breach-loading shotguns, Smith and Wesson double-actions, and goddamn you, we'll get you. I'll be damned if you ain't bound to go!"

Some merchants placed large orders for firearms. Rufus Hatcher, a carpenter, went to Vass's hardware store to buy some nails. While waiting for the clerk he overheard Vass being asked three times about his expected shipment of five hundred "Bulldogs." Hatcher was later told that these were "pistols that you don't have to cock at all, just as long as you pull, you keep firing."[41]

In an attempt to make Danville an issue across the state, the Third Ward Club prepared to distribute a political pamphlet ten days before the election. They intended to portray whites in the town as being dominated by blacks. Judge Aiken, a leading Democrat, told William Ruffin to write a draft. Aiken didn't like his work, thinking it to be too soft, and completely changed it. He then convinced twenty-eight of Danville's leading businessmen, including William Sutherlin, still a leading political and business figure twenty-eight years after the start of the Civil War, to sign it. Ruffin believed that the judge's version was inaccurate and full of exaggeration, but added his signature after he was told that it would help "carry Rockingham County and save all of the counties in the valley."[42]

41 Testimony of Squire Taliaferro, U.S. Senate; Testimony of J.J. Verser, U.S. Senate; Testimony of Rufus Hatcher, U.S. Senate.

42 Testimony of William Ruffin, U.S. Senate; U.S. Senate, p. X.

Virginia Democrats hoped that the circular would move whites to vote for their party and immediately distributed it everywhere in their state, except in Danville. It started out with two introductory paragraphs, which claimed that blacks, under the direction of William Mahone, had handpicked the city council. As a result, the public market lay ruined. Twenty out of twenty-four stalls were rented to blacks and now there was a "scene of filth with the stench of crowds loitering and idle Negroes, drunkenness, obscene language, and petit thieves." North Carolina tobacco planters now went "five times as far to a market in their own state on account of the Negro rule in the town."

That wasn't all. Two policemen had to be dismissed for embezzlement while blacks ran wild and terrorized the whites. "In several instances white children have been struck by grown Negroes," Aiken wrote. "We know of several cases where the lie has been given to a white lady to her face by a Negro." The circular ended with a plea to vote "in the cause of freedom to help up throttle this viper of Negroism that is stinging us to madness and to death, by voting against the Coalition-Radical candidates who are yelling and screaming with delight at the prospect of fastening its fangs into us forever."

Almost every point in the circular wasn't true. It was true that twenty of the twenty-four stalls were rented out to blacks, but this was not due to the influence of the city council, but due to the fact that they were auctioned off and black merchants happened to be the highest bidders. Neither had the conditions of the market changed for the worse. The tobacco business was harmed, not because of Readjuster rule, but because warehouses in Durham, North Carolina, began to pay more than Danville merchants for tobacco leaves. The only point that was accurate in the circular was that two policemen had been dismissed from duty.

Danville Judge John D. Blackwell, a Readjuster appointee, found the circular shocking. He registered his concerns in sharp language:

I have read this circular with mingled feelings of astonishment, sorrow, and indignation—astonishment and
sorrow at seeing the names of some persons of known
integrity and truth (if their signatures be not false) affixed
to a document containing so much falsehood, and these
elements so ingeniously commingled together that an
entire false impression is left upon the reader; and indignation that any class of men, however morally deprived
by nature or education, or however blinded by prejudice
and passion, should be so far lost to ordinary reason and
common sense as to endorse a paper which has been
evidently prepared for a political purpose by someone
who is regardless of truth.[43]

Unfortunately for the Readjusters, the accuracy of the individual statements in the circular was not as significant as the overall tone. Politically, the Democrats forced the Readjusters to leave
their issues behind them and defend themselves against the attacks, something difficult to do without making them appear to be
at least partly true. Mahone realized that the Danville Democrats
had put his party in a difficult position. The pamphlet is "designed
to excite the prejudices and passions of the white people at a
moment just before they are to vote, and to influence their votes
before they shall have time for reflection—before they shall have
time to enquire into the truthfulness of the statements made,"
he wrote.

The Readjusters couldn't denounce their own supporters.
Their only chance lay in refuting the circular immediately. For that
job, the party relied on Colonel W. E. Sims. Sims had fought in
the Confederate army and now worked as a lawyer in Chatham
where he became the Readjuster Party chairman for Pittsylvania
County and superintendent of its school system. Knowing the
area, he made himself the logical choice to come to Danville and

---

43 Melzer, pp. 33-35.

refute the pamphlet. When they learned of his trip, the town's Readjusters posted notices announcing his appearance.[44]

As Sims traveled to Danville, rumors of coming violence spread. While taking a train from Richmond to Martinsville, W. S. Jones heard of trouble brewing. His seatmate, who was traveling to Danville, told him that he had not expected to go back home for a few days. However, he received a telegram urging his return, because the racial situation had worsened. He then told Jones that he wasn't worried about the black Readjusters, because "three signals from the Star Warehouse bell would raise a hundred men at arms at anytime."[45]

That evening about five hundred people gathered, by the municipal building, to hear Sims speak. A. M. Wheeler, a white man and Danville Readjuster, delivered a speech urging everyone to keep the peace on Election Day. No one should go armed to the polls or provoke the Democrats, he said. After he finished, Squire Taliaferro approached the crowd and spoke to "kill time" until Sims arrived.

Once the crowd spotted Sims, they shouted in support as they watched him take the stage and prepare to speak. With the circular in hand, Sims slowly went through each of its points, taking them apart piece by piece. Afterward, Sims called the authors of the document cowards for slandering and vilifying blacks "when they knew how faithful the colored people had been to the Southern people during the late war; when they knew how respectful and polite the colored people were up to that time." He then read out the names of the people who signed the circular and branded them "willful and malicious liars."

The crowd began to murmur. Sims wasn't sure why they were stirring. A man approached the stage and told him that Joe Oliver, a captain of the Danville Grays, the local militia, had drawn his pistol and threatened to shoot Sims. Oliver and a group of Grays had the meeting surrounded.

---

44 Melzer, p.40; Tate, pp.62-66.
45 Testimony of W. S. Jones, U.S. Senate.

After a few minutes the crowd quieted down. Sims raised his hand and told them that he could settle the matter. He added that if the men wanted to shoot him then daylight is the place to do it and not a political meeting. "The men who sympathized with and espoused the cause of the Danville circular, which was filled with lies," he continued, "would not hesitate to stab a man in the dark or shoot him in the back." Sims noted that he "had never known a liar who was not a coward" and if anyone disputed what he said about the circular then stand up and correct him. No one did.

Sims concluded with a warning to his audience. "I told my constituents that I was satisfied that an effort was being made to create a race excitement so as to have difficulties on the day of the election," he later remembered, "yet I hoped that the colored people would refrain from even a sign of violence, that if any of them had any weapons they had better leave them at home, and stop wearing them; that if white people could afford to wear them there, I did not think the colored people could; that if a white man offered any of them any indignity or insult or violence up to or including the day of the election, they ought to pocket the insult, and bear the violence without saying one word, but go to the polls and vote their honest sentiments."

Danville's Democrats did not care to be called liars or cowards. As Sims finished his speech and stepped off the stage, a messenger from Mayor Johnston met him and informed him that if Sims went out on the streets he would be seized and lynched. The mayor offered to let Sims stay in his office until he could be safely escorted to his lodging.

Sims accepted and fled to the mayor's office. While he sat to pass time, Doctor R. V. Barksdale came into the office and identified himself as a spokesman for the Democrats. Sims later recalled that the doctor told him "that the men whom I had denounced as liars demanded a retraction; if I would go to the front of the building and take back all that I had said, he [Barksdale] was satisfied that he could quiet the crowd that night, and that I would not be killed, otherwise I would be." Sims refused and then left the office. Accompanied by friends, he went to his lodging and slept for the night.[46]

The Danville Riot

As the sun rose the next day, Saturday, November 3, 1883, the town reverberated with tension. In the morning, Wimbush Young, a white horse trader, noticed three black men talking on a corner. He recognized one of them as Elijah Cousins. "Elijah, come over here," Young called out.

As Cousins approached him, Young shifted the saddlebags on his shoulders and then looked at Cousins. "You get out of the street," Young told him, "and tell all of the boys from Jacksonville to get off the street, for some of them are going to get killed this evening." As Young left, Cousins studied him for a moment and decided that he had just heard nothing but more talk and rumors.[47]

William Mivins, a black barber, received a similar warning. While working in his shop, he was told to stay off the streets that day. Several white men brought new pistols into the shop and loaded them to give their order more emphasis. But he didn't think this unusual, for most men, white and colored, carried guns around at the time. Besides, business had been good that morning.[48]

At about 11:00 a.m., Granderion Poteat rested in the shade on Patton Street and listened to a conversation that made him uneasy. He had been putting away benches in his church and decided to sit and rest for an hour. As he lay out of sight in the shade of a small shed, he overheard John Edwards and Rufus Williams, two ex-policemen, talking.

"You go to Mr. Schoolfield's and get all he has got and from there to Colonel Grasty's store and get what he's got and I'll meet you at Mr. Joplin's myself and then we'll go from there to Captain Graves's house," Edwards said.

---

46 Melzer, pp.45-48; Testimony of William Sims, U.S. Senate.
47 Testimony of Elijah Cousin, U.S. Senate.
48 Testimony of William Mivins, U.S. Senate.

Poteat didn't understand what they were talking about. After the two men left, Poteat overheard two other white men as they passed by who made things clear to him.

"There's going to be hell to pay here directly," one said to the other.

"What is it?"

"We're going to fire on the niggers this evening," he replied.

After the two walked by, Poteat got up and crossed the street. He bumped into Captain Hall, the chief of police, and told him what he had just heard. Hall asked who the men were and Poteat pointed to two strangers who were leaving on horseback on a road that went to North Carolina. Hall said he didn't think anything would happen. But Poteat's worries didn't go away. "If it don't happen, I'll be right happy to see it, but I'm not going to dinner," he said.[49]

At the same time that Young warned Elijah Cousins, Colonel Sims woke up. His political aide, J. J. Verser, had awakened earlier and warned him that a crowd had gathered outside of the hotel and was threatening to shoot Sims. The colonel said that he wasn't concerned, because "cowards did not shoot men to their face in the daytime." He dressed and went down the stairs.

Sims found angry men waiting in the main hall and right outside of the door. Ignoring their threats, he walked past them and defiantly acted as if it was just a normal day. He went to a barbershop and got shaved. He then strolled over to a nearby restaurant and ate breakfast while Verser moved his buggy to the front of the building.

Sims left the restaurant and went inside an adjacent bar. After taking a drink, he went into the street and found himself confronted with a crowd of thirty white men who stood glaring at him with contempt. On the other side of the street one hundred fifty blacks stood and watched the whites. Sims walked toward the middle of the street, where his buggy sat. The white

---

49 Testimony of Granderion Poteat, U.S. Senate.

men were "scowling and looking at me with their hands in their pockets, holding hurried consultations, moving backward and forward in front of me and all around me," as he climbed into his buggy and left for Chatham, he later recalled.[50]

While Sims climbed into the buggy, Frank Corbett, a black clerk in Vass's hardware store, stood watching. Davis Lewellyn, a black tobacco worker, approached him. "I expect to see Colonel Sims interrupted. If they did," Lewellyn said, "there would have been a mob here. Have you a pistol?"

"Why?"

"It seems you don't understand what is going on," Lewellyn replied as he turned and walked away.

Corbett hung around the street for a few minutes and then went into the bar where he spotted Lewellyn sitting on a stool with a friend of his. "They were drinking right smart, both good friends of mine. I didn't care to be with them at the time I passed through and went into the rear-room," he recalled. In the back room he saw Hense Lawson, another black man, arguing with Captain Oliver of the Danville Grays. They "got to using some pretty rough language to each other and I took Hense," Corbett said, "and carried him out, asked him to quit, not to have any fuss, but he told me it seems I didn't understand what was going on; that they were expecting a fuss, and he had as many friends backing him as Oliver."[51]

Lewellyn came out of the bar and walked with Lawson down Main Street. Charles Noel, a white accountant, walked in their direction. He had planned to go to a dry goods store and buy a cover for his buggy. Noel later told what happened next:

I was passing down Main Street very rapidly and I passed two darkies; didn't know who they were, and after I had passed, I came very close to being tripped by one of the darkies whom I had passed by kicking my left foot; he came

---

50 Testimony of William Sims, U.S. Senate; Testimony of J. J. Verser, U.S. Senate.
51 Testimony of Frank Corbett, U.S. Senate.

very near to knocking my left foot from under me and I thought I was at least far enough from him not to trod on by them, and I turned and asked, "What did you do that for?" And he said, "I was only getting out of the way of a lady, a white lady at that," in a very insulting manner.

Noel replied by saying, "That's all right," and then continued walking.

"It don't make a damn bit o' difference whether it was all right or not," Lewellyn chided him, "you can't do anything about it!"

With that Noel turned and punched Lewellyn in the face.

"And then I struck him, they both struck me back and pushed me from the sidewalk, pushing me into the gutter," Noel recalled.

Noel jumped back onto the sidewalk and got ready to resume swinging. Then Lawson and Lewellyn made motions as if they were about to draw pistols out of their pockets. Noel ran down the street terrified.

After catching his breath, Noel went into a dry goods store and bought his buggy cover. He then went home, ate some dinner, and grabbed his pistol. He had heard that the Democrats were going to hold a meeting at the Opera House at 2:00 p.m. and didn't want to miss it.[52]

Back in town the meeting started right on schedule. Inside the Opera House the lower floor was packed, while the balcony, normally reserved for blacks, lay empty. Colonel George Cabell presided over the meeting as a young lawyer, H. E. Barksdale, read two resolutions to the audience.

The first resolution reaffirmed the validity of the circular drawn up by Judge Aiken, while the second resolution denounced William Sims. It also stated that if any violence came it would be his fault. Sims "delivered the most incendiary and inflammatory harangue ever delivered in a civilized community," the resolution

---

52 Testimony of Charles Noel, U.S. Senate; Testimony of Hense Lawson, U.S. Senate; Testimony of Davis Lewellyn, U.S. Senate.

said, "and as calculated, and is believed to have intended, to incite riot and bloodshed. At the same time the forbearance of our good citizens, who have thus far restrained their indignation, is an evidence of their desire to preserve the peace in this crisis if it can be reasonably done."[53]

As the meeting wrapped up, Noel entered the Opera House and spotted two of his friends, George Lea and William Taylor, standing in the gallery. Word had gotten around about Noel's encounter. Lea beckoned to him.

"What about the difficulty you had before dinner?" Lea asked him.

"It was a trifling affair. It don't make any difference now. I am going to the country, and am anxious to go, and wouldn't have any difficulty on this day, of course, as there are a great many darkies on the street, and it is best that we don't do anything about it."

Lea replied, "It's very hard to take an insult."

"Well, I've concluded to postpone it," Noel said, "as there is a very heated excitement in town. If we were to resent that injury it will bring a riot; I'll wait until after the election to resent the injury."[54]

Noel loitered for a few moments and then went back outside. He got into his buggy and began to trot up Main Street. As he went uphill and passed by the Arlington Hotel, Noel heard someone yell out, "By God, here I am!"

At first Noel couldn't tell where the voice came from. But then he spotted Lewellyn and Lawson standing together. Noel quickly turned his buggy around and went back down the hill. Looking back, he saw Lewellyn and Lawson slowly follow him with about twenty other black men behind them. Noel climbed out of the buggy and dashed into the Opera House.

Noel soon came out of the opera house with George Lea and William Taylor at his side. Walking toward Lawson, Noel bellowed out, "What did you mean by hailing me on the street?"

---

53 Melzer, pp.58-59; Testimony of H. E. Barksdale, U.S. Senate.
54 Testimony of Charles Noel, U.S. Senate; Testimony of George Lea, U.S. Senate.

Lawson stammered and denied that he yelled for him. With that Noel struck him in the face with a pair of brass knuckles. As Lawson fell to the ground Lea saw several other blacks begin to walk toward the scene. Wanting to see the fight continue without any interference, he quickly brandished a revolver and warned, "Stand back or I will shoot the last one of you niggers' heads off."[55]

A man on the other side of the street screamed, "Murder," drawing more people to the scene. Robert Adams, a black officer, was in Mr. White and Everett's store when he heard the man yell. He quickly walked out onto the street and saw Noel beating Lawson. "Lawyer Barksdale, one, lawyer Oliver was another, John Lea was one, and a man by the name of Bob Miller...had their pistols cocked, and a Mr. Noel was beating Hense with a slat or a stick, and had a bowie knife in his hand, and was beating him over the head with something," he later remembered. Adams walked up to the fight and tried to stop Noel. Jeff Corbin, a white man, came to help him, telling the people around the fight, "That man is an officer, let's part 'em."

While the two men separated Noel from Lawson, George Adams (no relation to Robert Adams), came out of the crowd and tried to take George Lea's pistol. He ran up behind Lea and tried to grab it. "When I started around," George Adams later recalled, "Mr. Lea cocked his pistol in my face and I grabbed it and tried to snatch it out of his hand." William Taylor hit Adams with a cane, and, as the two men struggled for the pistol, they fell. The pistol hit the ground and accidentally discharged. Adams jumped up and ran to the crowd of blacks. Pointing back at Lea, he yelled, "There was the damned rascal that had the pistol; if I had got it, I would have killed him!"[56]

Policeman Robert Adams recalled, "The shooting of that one pistol caused people to come from each side of the street, both

---

55 Testimony of Charles Noe, U.S. Senate; Testimony of Hense Lawson, U.S. Senate; Testimony of Davis Lewellyn, U.S. Senate; Testimony of George Lea, U.S. Senate.
56 Testimony of B. F. Williamson, U.S. Senate; Testimony of George Adams, U.S. Senate.

white and black, and I went up to the corner to blow my whistle, and sent over to the chief, who was at the mayor's office...if they didn't there would be a fuss out there." Soon, between one hundred fifty and two hundred blacks came to the scene. This didn't surprise Adams, because "They always do whenever they hear a policeman has a man. If a policeman has arrested a man, you will find before they get to jail, [people] will follow on going to see what you are going to do with them."[57]

After getting up from the ground, Lawson quickly composed himself and saw "several [white] men come out of the insurance office of Woolfolk and Blair, I think. I don't know exactly who it was; they were handing out guns right there from the insurance company." The whites and blacks began to argue with each other. In the commotion Lawson took off running down the street and hid inside a jewelry store.[58]

The crowd of blacks demanded that the police arrest Noel and the other whites for carrying concealed weapons. Robert Adams tried to calm the crowd and get both sides to leave, but some of the whites sneered at him. Joe Oliver told him, "We don't want none of your damn peace."

George Adams worried about Robert Adams and told him, "Bob, you get out of the crowd, because one of them men will kill you directly and you won't have any protection at all."

Robert Adams recalled that he then "looked at it and thought it over, and sort of stepped back." He knew most of the blacks were unarmed and didn't want to provoke the whites. "About two months before the election they held court in Danville and the grand jury indicted the old police force and everybody they knew for carrying pistols," he explained, "for carrying concealed weapons, and you know of course the colored people, being poor, they couldn't pay for carrying a pistol $15, $18, or $20 when they didn't have the money, and of course that scared them, and those that had been carrying pistols stopped."

57 Testimony of Robert Adams, U.S. Senate.
58 Testimony of Hense Lawson, U.S. Senate.

Robert Adams went into the crowd of blacks and told them, "You had all better leave here. Of course you ain't doing nothing to raise disturbance, but you better leave."

E. M. Hatcher, a white man, yelled, "Damn it, make these niggers get off the street."

Charles Freeman, a white cop, told Hatcher, "The colored people ain't doing nothing; if you all don't bother them they won't bother you."

Hatcher responded, "Damn it, we are going to kill all them and all their backers." Freeman got scared, told the blacks to leave, and then left.

A couple of the blacks yelled something to Hatcher. Hatcher then looked toward the crowd of blacks and yelled back, "This is a white man's town, and white men are going to rule it! I'll be damned if you niggers don't leave here, we are going to kill you!"[59]

W. R. Taylor heard someone in the crowd respond that "they could shoot just as good as the white people could, and if they shot to kill [they would shoot] the ones that started first." A few seconds later, Hatcher pointed a gun at the blacks and fired. Daniel Dugger, a white Democrat who watched as a bystander, said, "I saw Mr. Hatcher when he deliberately came off the sidewalk, walked in front of the niggers and told them to git, and when he did so, he turned and said, 'Boys, stand by me,' and when he did so he fired deliberately into the Negroes as they ran off."

Daniel Dugger, Robert Adams, and Jack Redd all testified that Hatcher fired the first shot. Hatcher later gave the following exchange under oath:

Q – Did you hear the command of fire given?
A – Yes, sir.

---

59 Testimony of Robert Adams, U.S. Senate; Testimony of Charles Freeman, U.S. Senate; Testimony of Daniel Dugger, U.S. Senate.

Q – Who gave the word?

A – I could not say positively who it was who gave it.

Q – Did you not give it?

A – I don't know whether I was the first one that gave it or not.

Q – At that time you were armed?

A – I was not.

Q – Are you sure you gave it?

A – I am not sure.

Q – Why did you give the word fire; you are uncertain whether you gave it or not?

A – I don't know whether I gave it at all or not.

Q – Was there any previous notice or warning given to the colored people?

A – Not that I ever heard of.

Q – What was the result of that fire—how many killed or wounded?

A – I didn't see but three that was killed.

Q – How many wounded?

A – I never saw but one man that was wounded.

Q – And you say you did not yourself fire any pistol or weapon into the crowd.

A – No sir, I didn't have any pistol that day.

Q – How many shots were fired?

A – I couldn't tell you that.

Q – About how many?

A – Oh, I have no idea how many was fired. I could not tell you.

Q – Did you see any persons firing?

A – I could not say that I did, I could not say I saw any whites or blacks fire; there was a pistol in the hands of good many... I am the poorest man in the world to recollect names.

Daniel Dugger said, "I believe today if Mr. Hatcher hadn't fired that pistol there would not have been any Negroes killed. I know he had a pistol. I understand Mr. Hatcher denied having a pistol, but I know as well as I know I am living, or know anything." [60]

Judge John D. Blackwell watched the scene unfold from the safety of his upper-level office window across from the Woolfolkand Blair store. With this vantage point he is the best witness to what unfolded. He said:

> I could see that Mr. Motley and Mr. Hatcher and two or three other whites, whom I did not recognize and do not know now, were apparently conversing in a very excited and angry manner with Negroes in the street. I could not hear what they said, but could see from the motion of their jaws and lips that they were in conversation with three or four Negroes in the street, who evidently replied to them in the same excited manner, as I inferred from their gesticulations, raising up their hands, but I could hear nothing, as I say.
>
> At that time the difficulty such as it was which I supposed was a street fight between a white man and Negro which frequently occurs in our streets, was at an end, when suddenly, to my surprise, I saw a line of whites, fifteen, possibly twenty—somewhere about that number—station themselves, a great majority upon the sidewalk, but several of them, so, three to six, perhaps out at the upper end of the street, out in the street, and they presented pistols.
>
> They suddenly presented pistols, and I heard the click; I was very much surprised at it; it was done so quickly. The Negroes there seeing the pistols or hearing them click, I don't know which, probably both, immediately turned as

---

60 Testimony of Charles Noel, U.S. Senate; Testimony of Davis Lewellyn, U.S. Senate; Testimony of George Lea, U.S. Senate; Testimony of Robert Adams, U.S. Senate; Testimony of E. F. Hatcher, U.S. Senate; Testimony of Daniel Dugger, U.S. Senate; Testimony of Jack Reed, U.S. Senate. Robert Adams, Jack Reed, and Daniel Dugger all testified that Hatcher fired the first shot.

quickly as they could and ran. By the time their backs were fairly turned—some of them I reckon had not been able to turn—the firing commenced. The discharge was a volley that was delivered as it had been by disciplined soldiers. I never on a battlefield heard a volley delivered as well together as that was. After that it was continuous firing, as if soldiers firing at will. Each man apparently shooting as quickly as he could, but to my astonishment I saw no effect from the bullets; no one seemed to be hurt at all. There were some shouts, some screams too, from the Negroes, as they ran, but that was apparently from fright. They ran nearly all of them down the street in the direction toward my right and below me...toward what I designate as South Market Street.

Evidently the great majority of them must have gone down that street, because they disappeared from my view so quickly, but a portion of them, when they got down to Market Street where it crosses Main—a few of them— evidently went down.[61]

George Adams recollected that, as he took off running, "Lea shot at me twice...and I ran about a hundred yards and they shot at me again, and another fellow was running at my side...named Jerry Smith, and he had run with me about a hundred yards, and they missed me and hit Jerry and Jerry fell right across the wall of a hardware store, and I turned right across and went across the alley to White's livery stable, and Mr. Pete Booth shot at me, and Mr. Hatcher say, 'there's that damn George Adams. I tried my best to kill him.'" Adams slipped out of view and later took off in his wagon.[62]

Granderion Poteat escaped by going into the Wiseman Drug Store. "As I started into the store his clerk remarked to me, 'Don't come in here, we will kill you,' and Mr. Wiseman came running and

---

61 Testimony of John Blackwell, U.S. Senate.
62 Testimony of George Adams, U.S. Senate.

says, 'Open the door and let everyone come in that can get in, and you all put those pistols down for I have nothing in the world to do with it,'" Poteat remembered.[63]

When the skirmish ended four blacks lay dead in the streets. As many as ten others were wounded, including one white man who had been accidentally shot and severely wounded while he fired off a pistol in each hand. He eventually died too.

Jack Redd, a black man who served as chairman of the Pittsylvania County Republican Party, had been in the crowd of blacks. He ran when he saw Hatcher cock his pistol. "I run, run over a wheel barrow and everything right down to the market," he recalled. "Well, after the firing was over I came walking back up the street with my hands in my pockets," he said. "To tell the truth I was noways scared, but I met Colonel Cabell right at the market."

While the two talked about trying to find a way to calm things down, Hatcher came up and asked Cabell, "Who is it?"

Cabell answered, "It is this damned scoundrel."

"Damn him, let me blow his damned brains out," Hatcher said.

Cabell replied, "No, let the damned scoundrel get out of town as fast as possible. This is what I've been telling you for the last ten years."

Hatcher struck Redd in the face. Redd turned around and took off running. Hatcher and another man fired their pistols at him. Cabell told them to stop and leave him alone. "They commenced firing at me again and I run down to the corner of the market, and by that time they got to firing at me. Just as I got there, I found out they were firing at me they quit," Redd recalled.[64]

The Danville Coup

Mayor J. H. Johnston first found out about the riot while resting at his home. His little girl came running into his house and told him of the shootings. Alarmed, he quickly went downtown where he

---

63 Testimony of Granderion Poteat, U.S. Senate.
64 Testimony of Jack Redd, U.S. Senate; Testimony of L. Ivery, U.S. Senate.

found Colonel Cabell speaking to a large crowd of "some three hundred men running up and down the street with guns, pistols, and bowie knives." Wanting to get control of the situation, the mayor sent someone to ring the Star Warehouse bell to signal the militia companies to come out.

Cabell approached the mayor and told him to make sure that the Douglas Guards, a local all-black militia company, didn't muster, because if the Douglas Guards did, the white men "would kill the last damned one of them." Frightened, Johnston told Police Chief Hall to tell all of the militia units to stay put. When Hall returned, Cabell made sure he knew who was really in control by telling him, "Young man, make yourself small. Now I've just kept the crowd from mobbing you, just now."[65]

As the head of the local Democratic Party, Cabell took the lead of the mob. By sundown, under the pretense of defending the town from a black uprising, armed Democrats in groups of ten to fifteen men patrolled the streets.

Democrats in Danville quickly realized that they were faced with the quandary of explaining the chaos to people outside of the town. It wasn't a difficult problem to fix. They simply made sure that they were the first to present the story of the shooting and its aftermath by sending telegrams throughout the state's newspapers that said, "We are standing in our doors with shotguns in hand, defending our wives and children from an organized mob of Negroes now parading the streets." Rumors spread, perhaps intentionally, that it was the whites who were the ones killed.[66]

Other Virginia Democrats had no problem believing the story. In Lynchburg, Virginia, John W. Daniel and General Jubal Early held a mass meeting of Democrats to discuss the riot. Early best summed up the consensus. For him it was an unfortunate, but

65 Testimony of J. H. Johnston, U.S. Senate.
66 Testimony of Melzer, p. 77; Tate, p. 105.

necessary, incident, because "The Negroes must know that they are to behave themselves and keep in their proper places."[67]

Democrats in other parts of the state agreed. The *Wytheville Times* blamed Mahone for the bloodshed and urged whites "to be true to their own race in the race conflict which Mahone has brought about."[68]

In Richmond, a Democratic meeting passed resolutions sympathizing with the white men in Danville and resting "all the responsibility for blood that may be shed or spilled by men who are driven to the conflict in the interest of civilization" on William Mahone.[69]

The editor of the *Lynchburg Times* published his thoughts:

We commend the white people of Danville for their course in their late unpleasantness. It was a desperate case and required a desperate remedy. If a row occurs here tomorrow, and I am sorry to say it may occur at any time, don't shoot the poor Negroes down, as was done in Danville, but commence at the office-holders first and kill down every devil of them. We intend to rule Virginia from this vile horde of Mahone radicals. It matter not what it may cost. The election is ours, and as sure as the sun goes down on tomorrow night, you will see, my friends, that Virginia will be relieved by the best people.[70]

W. P. Robinson came to Danville the evening after the riot and saw the real situation with his own eyes. Robinson had been in Sycamore Station, some fifty miles from Danville that afternoon. Having heard that blacks had taken over the streets, he became concerned about some rental properties he had in the town and

---

67 Charles Pearson, *The Readjuster Movement in Virginia* (New Haven: Yale University Press, 1917), p.164.

68 U.S. Senate, p.27.

69 Melzer, p.78.

70 U.S. Senate, p.XXXV.

headed straight for them. After he arrived, Robinson saw armed groups of white men patrolling the streets. "It occurred to me that it was the most foolish thing I ever seen in my whole life—the crowd to patrol that town—when I was satisfied that these Negroes were the worst broken up, they were the most demoralized, broken up, completely crushed, that they had no idea of raising arms or anything else against the white people," he recalled.[71]

Mayor Johnston and Judge Blackwell also walked the streets that evening. According to Johnston, they found "ten or fifteen men at every corner, on horses, cavalry...They were there they said, protecting their property, but I couldn't understand that, because the Negroes, those that had not left town had gone somewhere, they could not be seen...and I could not see any sense in it."

With the election only two days away, Johnston came to the conclusion that Colonel Cabell had taken control of the city and was using the mob to intimidate voters. Fearing that more violence would break out, the mayor sent a telegram to the governor asking for help, which read, "A riot occurred here this afternoon... the military are on duty and quiet for the present prevails. I, however, fear another outbreak before the election is over, and hope that you will send me a company of troops as speedily as possible. Our people are so excited that I do not think that they can be safely depended on to preserve order and keep down the riot."

The next morning Johnston received a note from William Sims, who had arrived in town, asking him if he intended to do anything to ensure that there would be a free election. The mayor sent a messenger back to Sims who told him that Colonel Cabell had taken over and he couldn't do anything at the moment. He also warned Sims to get out of town because he thought the mob would kill him if they found him. Sims left and traveled toward Richmond to get the assistance of Governor Cameron.

Mayor Johnston wired the governor:

---

71 Testimony of W. P. Robinson, U.S. Senate.

Citizens here are terrorizing the election with the pretense of patrolling the street and the roads beyond the corporate limits. I have not a force of sufficient strength to repress this disorder. The same spirit that caused the riot of yesterday prevails in unabated force, and in case of another outbreak, I think that the majority of the troops here will fraternize with the riot. The election on Tuesday will be a mere farce unless the electors are assured of protection at the polls by the foreign troops.

Governor Cameron answered back:

I am averse to the use of outside military except upon actual necessity. Answer at once and give particulars.

Johnston replied with particulars:

Out of abundant caution, we advise a military company from Lynchburg to be sent here this evening. Lynchburg is our nearest point and we want a company before night.

The governor answered this by advising that they stick with local forces:

If the present spirit of your community is such as your dispatches lead me to believe, there should be no difficulty in forming a posse of citizens whose coolness and desire to preserve the peace would effect more good than the sending of troops from elsewhere. Of course, in the face of your official statements, that actual violence is again threatened by any element of the community, and that the civil authorities have not the force to preserve the peace, I will promptly reinforce them in execution of the law. Advise me at once and fully of any change in the situation.

With few options left, the mayor and Judge Blackwell decided to ask Cabell to order the people off of the streets. But this went nowhere, because Cabell claimed that he no longer had anything to do with the situation.

Johnston went back to his office and decided to draw up a statement for the next day that would announce that he would take control of the town by appointing special constables to patrol the streets.[72]

The next morning, William Sims arrived at the governor's mansion and asked to speak with him. The governor sent a message telling Sims that he had not gotten dressed yet and to come back later. Yet, with the election only a day away, time was beginning to run out. Sims urgently dashed him a note:

> Dear Governor: I have just arrived from Danville. The condition there surpasses any reports that may have reached you. An armed mob still controls the town— Negroes are driven out—not allowed to come on the streets. I have no idea how a colored man can vote tomorrow. The Funder mob were parading the streets at eleven last night, with shotguns, rifles, etc., and firing could be heard in every part of the town. Nothing but United States troops can restore quiet or give our voters courage to come to the polls.

After he read the note, the governor dressed quickly and came down the stairs to meet Sims, where the two talked at length. Sims later recalled telling the governor that "no state troops would be of any service; that if they were colored troops, it would only bring on the war of races in Danville, and if they were white Democrat troops, the chances were that they would sympathize with the mob in Danville, and would only further intimidate the colored people."

---

72 Testimony of J. H. Johnston, U.S. Senate; Testimony of John Blackwell, U.S. Senate; Testimony of William Sims, U.S. Senate; Melzer, pp.75-77.

Governor Cameron told Sims that he would send troops by nightfall. However, he wouldn't say if they would be state militia or Federal troops. Sims had no choice but to hope for the best.[73]

As dawn came the next day in Danville, Monday, November 5, 1863, Mayor Johnston woke to read the *Danville Register*. In it he read a lead editorial that stated that if any disturbance occurred tomorrow on Election Day that "they hoped that no innocent men would suffer, but that the blood of the leaders should be shed." The editorial terrified some of its readers. The Readjusters who had been chosen to help oversee the election polls announced their resignation. Some Readjuster supporters left and never came back to Danville.

By afternoon the mob grew tired of walking the streets and thinned out. Johnston appointed special constables and called into service the Danville Grays white militia unit. He then posted a proclamation:

> I feel fully warranted in assuring my fellow-citizens that peace and good order will be maintained; and I, therefore, call upon all good citizens to resume their usual vocations; to cease appearing upon the streets armed with shotguns or other weapons, and thus, by quiet conduct and conversation—the things which make for peace—aid and assist me and the other authorities of the town in restoring peace and good order, as all good citizens should do.

A few hours later, Danville's leading Democrats, Readjusters, and businessmen issued a statement promising a free election. Among its signatories were Judge Blackwell, Colonel Cabell, Judge Aiken, Mayor Johnston, and J. B. Raulston. Once nightfall came, the mayor demobilized his special constables and ordered the Danville Grays to remain on active duty in the armory. By 9:00

---

73 Testimony of William Sims, U.S. Senate; Melzer, p. 79.

p.m. he received a cable from Governor Cameron telling him that troops were on the way.[74]

The next morning, November, 6, 1883, marked the dawn of Election Day. Virginia state militia troops arrived at 5:00 a.m. They relieved the Danville Grays and stayed at the armory for the rest of the day. However, they did little to reassure the supporters of the Readjusters who believed that they were in cahoots with the Democrats. D. W. Penhill, the secretary of the Readjusters for Pittsylvania County, wrote William Mahone telling him that the troops were nothing but a farce and commented that "Soldiers of no sort were necessary except regulars under the command of a determined officer like Sheridan clothed with the full power to declare martial law—try the ruffians and their instigators by a drumhead court martial and hang them immediately in a gallows extending the full length of Main Street—anything less than that would only aggravate the trouble and not remove it."[75]

While the state troops sat in the armory, most black and Readjuster voters remained too intimidated to vote. Nelson Scott, a former slave and Readjuster supporter, went to the Ringold voting district, seven miles outside of Danville. He cast his vote and then spent a few hours at the polls. There he witnessed the arrival of five or six Danville Democrats in buggies. As the men got out and walked toward the polling area, Scott noticed pistols sticking out of their pockets. He decided to leave the area and went home.[76]

W. P. Graves, a prominent Democrat who took part in the Danville riot, noticed that few blacks voted. He visited several precincts where he saw blacks watch the polls by peering out of windows or by standing back at a remarkable distance. He didn't see any of them cast a ballot and for good reason. Out of the town's 1,301 registered black voters only 31 voted that day. White Readjusters stayed home too, as the Democrats scored a

74 Testimony of J. H. Johnston, U.S. Senate; Melzer, pp. 80-83.
75 Tate, p. 97.
76 Testimony of Nelson Scott, U.S. Senate; Tate, p. 108.

resounding victory in Pittsylvania County. Out of 903 votes cast, Sims received only twenty-six. In the North Danville precinct all 200 votes went to Democrats in what turned out to be the greatest political landslide in the city's history.[77]

Yet the climate of fear did not end with the election. In its aftermath many white voters felt it necessary to recant their support for the Readjuster Party. Several of them sent notices to the *Danville Register:*

> I desire to say that, notwithstanding I have been heretofore classed with the Readjuster Party (which charge I do not deny), I am a white man, and shall in the future act with the Democratic Party in all elections, as I consider the question of Readjustment settled.—Respectfully R. E. Lee.

> To the public: I now take my stand in the Democratic Party to uphold the standard against the black flag of radicalism, as I ever did when in the Readjuster Party— Barker's notice.

> I wish to inform the people of Danville that I am a white man, and a Democrat and I am not a new convert. I have been a Democrat all the time and I have never pretended to be anything else but a Democrat. —W.A. Cook.[78]

In this atmosphere the Readjuster and independent members of the city council, including the mayor, and the black policemen, announced their resignations before the election. Some of them fled town never to return. J. B. Raulston left, announcing, "In view of recent events, I do not think that I can any longer be useful as a member." Davis Lewellyn moved to New York City. George Cabell and the local Democrats handpicked the successors of those who left. One of them, whom they chose to serve on city

---

77 Testimony of W. P. Graves, U.S. Senate; Melzer, p. 85; Tate, p. 113.
78 U.S. Senate, p.427.

council, Harry Wooding, later would serve as mayor of Danville for over thirty-eight years.[79]

Outside of Danville, the riot became the key issue for the state election. Two days before the election, the *Danville Register* published an account of the riot, which was reprinted throughout the state. According to the paper, while the Democrats were meeting to endorse the Danville circular and denounce Sims, a crowd of blacks gathered outside the Opera House to ridicule them. This jeering led to "a difficulty" between a young white man and a black man, the latter being "severely punished." Afterward, several Negroes "drew pistols, and dared the white men, who had also gathered around the scene, come on...One of the Negroes fired a pistol into a group of five white men and thereupon a fuselage of firearms ensued, in which about one hundred shots were fired. The Negroes scattered in every direction and the white men held their ground. Three Negroes were killed and two were wounded, one of whom will probably die."[80]

Democrats throughout the state tapped into white anxieties of black violence and old fears of slave insurrections by using the story of the riot as political propaganda, contrasting a vote for the Democrats as a vote for rule by whites and a vote for the Readjusters as a vote a vote for more bloodshed and black tyranny. A circular titled "Riot in Danville," distributed throughout southwest Virginia, placed responsibility for the riot on the "diabolical speeches by the Mahone nihilists" and commented about the blacks in Danville, "Let the incendiary devils be crushed beyond the hope of resurrection."

A Lynchburg printing press operated nonstop up until Election Day, printing a pamphlet written by Jubal Early that was sent all over the state. In it the general expressed sympathy for the people of Danville "in their struggle against the domination

79 Testimony of Charles Freeman, U.S. Senate; Edward Pollock, *Illustrated Sketch Book of Danville, Virginia: Its Manufacturers and Commerce*, reprint edition (Danville: The Danville Historical Society, 1976), p.73.
80 Tate, p.105.

of the Negro race under the lead of renegade white men whose hearts are blacker than the skins of their unfortunate dupes." It continued, "Virginia is white man's country, and we are determined that our Mother state shall not be ruled by thieves, liars, and cowards with white faces by the aid of their allies, the colored people."

The propaganda worked. Four days after the election the ballots were officially counted. Out of 267,000 votes, the Democrats won an 18,000-vote majority. Mahone's supporters blamed their loss on the riot. P. H. McCaull of Salem wrote Mahone, "The Danville riot and funder lies defeated us. They are welcome to victories obtained that way." Another ally from Faugueir County informed Mahone:

> The Danville affair was gotten up in circulars containing the most brazen and outrageous lies by the tens of thousands, they run their printing presses here all day last Sunday and at least a dozen horsemen starting to every neighborhood in this and Craig counties and by Monday night the people in remote settlements, especially the ignorant classes, was worked up to believe that the whole state was overridden if the Readjuster was successful. And I have no doubt this scheme was carried out all through the Southwest.

Mahone at first remained optimistic, telling allies, "We are badly beaten, but not dismayed." However, he shortly disbanded the Readjuster Party and eventually went into retirement. In the end the general felt remorse about the whole affair, saying, "I feel guilty of having unintentionally and unwillingly...given them (the colored people) advice which was seized on by their political enemies to slaughter them." W. P. Robinson thought it "was the worst I ever saw in any civilized country." For Democrats, though, the election marked the beginning of almost a century of their party's control of Virginia.[81]

For many Democrats the rise of Mahone and existence of black voters proved that Virginia had too much democracy. Too many people were allowed to vote and the only way to keep them in line was through means such as the Danville riot. It would be better to eliminate this problem by removing people from the voting rolls altogether rather than resort to such distasteful measures again. An editorial in the Richmond Dispatch argued that "every step toward pure democracy in the states has increased the depravity in the political arena...any backwards step that may re-establish conservative checks upon the corruptions of demagoguism will protract the duration of republicanism." The Richmond State agreed, stating, "The true teaching is that both caste and class must exist in all organized society, and their abolition, admitting such a thing possible, could result in nothing else but a return to primitive barbarism, for they are the outcome of civilization."[82]

Democrats called for a constitutional convention that would disenfranchise blacks. Their resolutions were voted down twice, but in 1901 the voters finally consented. John W. Daniel, Carter Glass, William Cameron, and John Goode of Bedford were among those elected to convene it. Daniel chaired the convention, but due to illness, Carter Glass took up most of his duties.

Glass intended to eliminate as many black voters as possible. He claimed that black voting was "a crime to begin with and a wretched failure to the end" and that "the unlawful but necessary expedients employed to preserve us from the evil effects of the thing were debauching morals and warping the intellect of our own race." Once finished, the new constitution stipulated that all voters had to pay three years' worth of a poll tax, a fee

---

81 Jane Dailey, Before Jim Crow: The Politics of Race in Postemancipation Virginia (Chapel Hill: University of North Carolina Press, 2000), p.150; Tate, pp.104-118, 131.

82 C. Van Woodward, Origins of the New South: 1877-1913 (United States: Louisiana State University Press, 1951), p.53.

of $1.50 per year, no small sum in the early twentieth century, fill out a written application with the registrar, and have the ability to answer any questions the registrant may have "affecting his qualifications." The poll tax, however, had to be paid at least six months before an election, long before most people were interested in voting.

Blacks were hardly the only ones affected. The new voting requirements ended up disenfranchising most white voters, who were too poor to pay the poll tax also. In the next election the number of votes cast fell in half and steadily fell with each following election. Between 1925 and 1945 only 11.5 percent of the adult population in Virginia voted in her elections. Until the 1960s, political machines, which helped pay the poll taxes of their supporters and dispensed favors to them in return for their votes, dominated Virginia politics and spread voter apathy. Voting became an exercise for the well connected. When asked why she didn't vote, one woman from Lynchburg responded, "Elections are a foregone conclusion." Francis Miller, who ran for governor in 1949, remembered asking a painter in his neighborhood whom he had voted for. "Colonel," he answered, "you know I don't belong to the folks who vote."[83]

As the number of voters declined, the power to promote candidates to office became concentrated into fewer and fewer hands. But just as important for Danville, the riot created a visible rift in the town's community. Blacks, former white Readjusters, and Democrats had to find a way to pick up the pieces and move on with life.

For guidance, leading blacks and Readjusters in Staunton, Virginia, invited Revered J. Hudson Riddick to preach a special sermon about the riot on November 10, 1883, exactly a week

---

83 Dabney, p.436; V. O. Key, Jr., *Southern Politics in State and Nation* (Knoxville: University of Tennessee Press, 1996), pp.19-20; Robert Gooch, *The Poll Tax in Virginia Suffrage History: A Premature Proposal for Reform(1941)* (Charlottesville: Institute for Government, University of Virginia, 1969), pp.12-14; *Richmond Times-Dispatch*, May 12, 1946; *Washington Post*, June 11, 1957.

after it happened. Known throughout the land as a distinguished minister and speaker, he attracted an audience sprinkled with blacks and whites that filled the Methodist Episcopal Church to listen to him.

Insisting that he was speaking not as a racist, politician, or even a Methodist, but as a minister of the Lord, Riddick spoke of "death and its long black list of attendant woes to the human family." He warned, "Human life is too precious to be sacrificed by mobs and violence, or at the bidding of passions and prejudice from any quarter." Riddick continued:

> We have a large number of ignorant voters in the South, black and white. What we need is a baptism of education, not of blood and just so long as the people of the South continue to spell Negro with a small n, two g's, and an i, just so long will the South remain in the rear, and her able sons and daughters remain unprotected. To neglect education is to convert the Commonwealth into a volcano, more to be dreaded than the fires of Vesuvius. Ignorance is a danger signal, education a safety valve to the state and nation.

Riddick blamed the Danville "circular," on a "lawless few who assembled in a star-chamber, worse than any of those of Henry VIII...There was no riot in Danville; all accounts agree that the blacks were unarmed, and that they made no opposition, but were running away from the scene of disturbance. These six men were thus murdered."

"Their murderers," he continued, "must take their place in history with Cain and Judas, Booth, and Guiteau; and Danville in the future must be classed with Hamburg, Fort Pillow, and the bloody soil of Mississippi, Louisiana, and Texas." Riddick then assured the congregation that "these murderers" had surely violated the laws of God and man and said that history would someday judge Danville in the harshest manner. He then ended with a plea directed to the blacks of Virginia:

> Let us not cultivate a spirit of acrimony, revenge or bitterness, but a spirit of amity and forbearance. Let us trust in God for protection and deliverance. He will avenge the blood of these men in due time. Be true to God, true to yourselves, and true to your country, for "righteousness exalteth a nation, but sin is a reproach to any people." Take God as your captain and God's truth as your banner.

After Riddick spoke, the people of Staunton held a memorial service for the victims of the riot.[84]

On the same day that Riddick delivered his sermon, Danville's Democratic leaders met in the Opera House to discuss their own concerns. The riot gave the city negative press throughout the country. The *Pennsylvania Lancaster and Express*, for instance, charged that "the conduct of the Bourbon-Democrats in Virginia during the last two months settled it, that no man, no white man, can live in that state and maintain his self-respect... The Virginia 'gentleman' has written himself down during the past two months a liar and a swindler." Some newspaper accounts printed in the North disputed the local Democrats' version of the riot, claiming that the whole affair had been planned in advance. Danville's Democrats decided to counter these charges.[85]

The meeting in the Opera House concluded with the attendees agreeing to a appoint a "committee of forty, who shall be charged with the duty of thoroughly enquiring into all the facts and preparing for publication a true and full statement of the causes and circumstances which led to it, and also a statement of conduct of our people during the period from the occurrence of the riot to the closing of the polls on the 6th day of November."

---

84 Tate, p. 120-122.
85 Ibid., p. 117.

The committee appointed Major William Sutherlin as their chairman.

Sutherlin divided the committee into subcommittees and requested, through the *Danville Daily Register*, anyone with information about the riot to appear at the office of F. F. Bowen, a notary public, to have their statements heard and transcribed. Over the course of the next eleven days, the committee received the testimony of thirty-seven witnesses who were present on Main Street during the shooting.

After the final witness gave his story, Sutherlin summarized the findings of the committee and wrote its report. It declared that the blacks, because of their political success, had become "rude, insolent, and intolerant" toward white people. Colonel Sims provoked them to savagery as two blacks insulted a white man into a fight. This encounter excited the blacks to such a degree that they, "with loud exclamations and great violence of manner, forced upon the whites the conflict known as the Danville riot. All of the whites who fired upon the blacks did so in self-defense."

The report also claimed that, thirty minutes after the riot, the city was in complete control. The election that followed was "without any disturbance or difficulty...free and fair in all respects... the Negroes as a whole refrained from voting" as a result of advice given to them by their party leaders. The report concluded with the signatures of the committee members swearing to its validity and with a plea that it be accepted as "a full and complete vindication of our town and people from the gross misstatements which have been circulated."[86]

Predictably, the committee's report did little to convince people outside of Danville. The *Richmond Whig* stated that its findings were a "white-washing of the bleeding stain," and remarked, "The wolves testify and the verdict is that the sheep were guilty,

---

86 Committee of Forty, *Danville Riot: November 3, 1883* (Richmond: Kohns R. Coolsby, Book and Job Printers, 1883).

although killed and devoured." Some hoped that justice would come from the courts.[87]

When the circuit court began its next term, Judge Blackwell ordered a grand jury to investigate the circumstances surrounding the riot, an action that prompted the *Danville Register* to proclaim, "A short while ago the Democrats of Danville were a unit and red hot. Young and old, rich and poor, all were up to a fever heat. It is time now to steam up again for another fight. The object will be to rid Danville of every vestige of Negro rule. One more effort of the great Democratic stomach will throw up every particle of Radical stuff, which was left after the great upheaval in November last. Let's go to work, right away friends, and, if necessary, let us make it hotter than it was before."

After two sessions the judge announced that there would be no indictments, as the jury, packed with local Democrats, ruled that all the whites had fired in self-defense. In a twist of justice, George Myers, who served as jury foreman, released a fantastic statement drawn up by the jury, which portrayed the men under investigation as heroes:

> There was a determination on the part of the crowd of Negroes assembled to intimidate the whites by threats and menacing, that the effects of the policeman...and others were unsuccessful in prevailing upon the Negroes to disperse; that they persisted in remaining upon the scene of the fight, and giving expression to remarks calculated to excite the passions of the whites; that at last the whites fired off their pistols in the air, hoping hereby to cause the crowd to disperse; that the Negroes did not then dispense but rushed the scene from all quarters, advancing upon the whites with drawn pistols; that firing thereupon commenced; that the whites used their firearms in defense of their lives; that the whites were in imminent danger, and by their courage and pluck in

87 Tate, pp. 124-125.

standing up against such odds, saved the lives of hundreds of people in this city.[88]

Preston Watkins, who served on the jury, later said that he never expected to get at the truth. "I tried to some extent, but didn't believe in my own opinion that we would get any nearer," he said. "I don't know whether they were afraid to tell the truth, but I saw we was not getting any deeper than when we commenced." The only evidence the jury looked at came from the Committee of Forty's Report. "I was going by the evidence; I could not do anything more than the evidence," Watkins remarked. He remembered he wanted "to get off it as soon as possible," and "would agree to anything to get off."[89]

Angered by the events in Danville and the outcome of the court investigation, General Mahone lobbied to get the United States Congress to investigate the riot. In February 1883, the House Committee of Privileges and Elections launched a probe into it. Calling over 160 witnesses, the investigators' final report concluded that the riot threw the state election to the Democrats. The document blamed white Democrats in Danville for instigating it and concluded, "No punishment will probably ever be inflicted upon the perpetrators of this foul wrong in Danville." The investigation failed to persuade everyone, as Democrats seized on the fact that most of the congressmen on it were Republicans and claimed that it was nothing but a partisan witch-hunt. In Danville, memories colored the story of the riot, which took on a life of its own apart from the congressional investigation and even the local committee's report.[90]

As the years passed, people in Danville remembered the riot not through congressional investigations, but in accounts written by local writers, which blamed the riot on outside forces. In their view, neither local blacks nor white Democrats were to blame. Instead, northern carpetbaggers and outside agitators were.

---

88 U.S. Senate, p.429; Pollock, p.98; Tate, p.125.
89 Testimony of Preston Watkins, U.S. Senate.
90 Tate, p.126; U.S. Senate, pp.I-X.

For example, according to Jane Hagan, who wrote *The Story of Danville*, the riot was "caused by outside political forces and set off by incendiary agents." Mahone's agents exploited "ignorant Negroes." Without his meddling in local affairs, race relations would have remained friendly. It was a problem of the past. "Throughout the Reconstruction period the town struggled back toward happier times," Hagan wrote, "and without outside interference all might have gone smoothly. But as lightning clears the atmosphere on a sultry summer evening, the tragedy of the 'Danville Riot' came as the culmination of that time." Once local control had been restored "racial harmony and good feeling prevailed," she concluded.[91]

Edward Pollock, who wrote one of the first books on Danville, blamed the riot on Sims. He claimed that race relations were fine until the Readjusters took power. Once the Democrats got back in control "complete harmony between the races was speedily restored and has subsisted continuously since that time, with marked satisfaction to all parties concerned. I feel there is no town in the country where a better understanding prevails between capital and labor, employer and employed, white and colored, Democrat and Republican, than in Danville," he wrote.[92]

The white people of Danville who had supported the Readjusters were forgotten in these local accounts. They also inaccurately placed blame on Reconstruction, which had come to an end over a decade before the riot took place. However faulty the memory of the riot may have been, it played an important symbolic role in Danville throughout the first half of the twentieth century.

The parable of the riot was used by the city's leaders to teach the white people of Danville two important lessons. First, they had to be wary of abandoning the Democratic Party or listening to political leaders from outside the town. Secondly, they needed to understand that subverting the order of white supremacy would bring violence and chaos to the community. The only way to

---

91 Jane Hagan, *The Story of Danville* (New York: Stratford House, 1950), p. 18.
92 Pollock, p. 99.

maintain peace and harmony would be to keep blacks down and to allow the proper white leaders to rule. When the city's white textile workers would later go on strike in 1929, the *Danville Register* warned that it was the worst thing to happen since the riot.[93]

Jubal Early had been correct. The election was about placing blacks in their proper places and reminding whites that they needed to defer to the local elites in the Democratic Party. As local author Edward Pollock wrote, after the crisis of the riot passed, "Those who had been formerly most insolent in their conduct now became polite and respectful, ready to yield all reasonable deference to their natural superiors, and to resume, contently, their own legitimate position in the social scale." In the following years, Democrats worked to make this social order permanent by putting it into law, first by passing segregation laws and then by rewriting the Virginia Constitution to disenfranchise tens of thousands of voters.[94]

For city leaders the riot became something not to be ashamed of, but to celebrate. Forty years after the riot, the *Danville Register* dedicated an entire issue to remembering the event and putting it into perspective. Heading off any criticisms, the paper stated, "While some have expressed a fear that such a revival of an old story may revive old antagonisms and impair the highly satisfactory inter-racial relations now existing, we think such anticipation is entirely groundless. The whole affair is history." The paper found nothing that reflected unfavorably upon the white residents of the city at the time. Instead, "their self-control and forbearance and the courageous calmness with which they met and mastered a great emergency are notable and probably deterred and prevented other such clashes." The paper concluded:

It appears to the thoughtful observer that the subsequent action of the constitutional convention of 1901–1902 in

93 William Mainwaring, Jr., *Community in Danville, Virginia, 1880-1963* (Ph.D. dissertation, The University of North Carolina at Chapel Hill, 1988), pp.75-77.
94 Pollock, p.99.

eliminating the violent, the thriftless, and the ignorant of both races from the electorate has operated to the well being of the colored people of the state than to their injury; we venture to say that in no other city in the country are the thrift, welfare, and character of its Negroes more noteworthy than in Danville.

Like Pollock, newspaper editors attributed this latter point to the lessons the blacks of Danville learned from the riot, an event the paper called a "stirring chapter in the city's history" and a "thrilling clash."[95]

The Legacy of the Danville Riot

The riot itself is an example of the factionalism that is inherent in all societies. The ascendancy of the Readjusters of Danville upset the local power structure. Those who owned the largest businesses and the most property in town had provided the community with its principal leadership. Now they found themselves challenged and pushed aside with little chance of regaining their power through a fair election. The only way they could restore their traditional role was through fear and intimidation.

As the riot faded into the past, city leaders used it throughout the first half of the twentieth century as a testament to their rule, connecting it with white supremacy. Once white supremacy became disreputable, people could no longer think of the riot as a moving story or use it as a parable to defend the status quo. It then disappeared from the city's collective consciousness and became a trivial antiquarian event of the past, known by few and commemorated by no one.

However, from the day of the riot, Danville's Democrats consciously tried to control outside perceptions of the event. Local historians portrayed Danville as a place of no animosity and praised its social order. Violence was not caused by anyone

---

95 Mainwaring, p.74; Danville *Register*, March 11, 1923.

living in Danville, they claimed. Instead, violence was the result of outsiders who came to town and stirred people up by giving them misleading ideas about who they should be. Myths serve a purpose, and in this case the blaming of outside agitators had the effect of leaving Danville's Democrats blameless while serving as a warning to those who thought of stepping out of line.

They were hardly alone in Southern myth-making. Many Southerners tried to control how the past was remembered. General Jubal Early and like-minded allies took over the Southern Historical Society and promoted books and articles that portrayed the Confederate defeat in the Civil War as a noble "Lost Cause." At a founding meeting of the SHS, Early argued that the Confederate soldiers never lost on the battlefield, but rather that mass numbers and endless resources simply had defeated them. He claimed that secession was right and honorable. The cause of the war had to be advanced. At this "bar" of history, said Early, Southerners had to be shown "as patriots demanding our rights and vindicating the true principles of the government founded by our fathers."[96]

The pages of the SHS's journals argued that slavery was right and that blacks actually suffered from emancipation. Writers such as Thomas Nelson Page wrote sentimental stories of slave times, in which slaves were honored as loyal servants, while their masters were seen as archetypes of benevolence. The plantation was a loving family. Page's slaves found the end of the Civil War as a lonely and bewildering time.[97]

The "Lost Cause" and sentimental plantation stories also led to an interpretation of Reconstruction that was identical to the way Democrats explained the Danville Riot. Democrats across the South portrayed themselves as redeemers who freed their land from the oppression of corrupt Northern "carpetbaggers,"

---

96 Blight, p.79
97 Ibid., p. 222.

traitorous local "scalawags," and childlike blacks unprepared for freedom and in need of white rule.[98]

In reality the people of the Northern states were never wholly united behind the Civil War and neither were the people of the Confederacy. The period after the Civil War was not one of Union oppression against the South, but one that saw the South divided against itself over the course of its own future. When Democrats took power over Danville and the state of Virginia, they used white supremacy and "Lost Cause" nostalgia to bury divisions among whites and justify their own rule.

White supremacy was the only issue that Democrats could use to bring white voters together. The Readjusters showed that any other issue could tear the party apart or cause a second party to win. It took violence to maintain white supremacy and keep all people in line.

John Moffett, a white Danville minister, learned that lesson the hard way. In 1887, Moffett became the minister to the Missionary Baptist congregation in North Danville. Within two years he increased the size of his congregation fivefold and raised money to build a larger church. People respected his drive and ambition. One fellow Baptist minister said of him that he worked "like a beaver, always on the outlook for newcomers, with a happy faculty for recognizing people and for putting them to work."

At the time Prohibition was a popular reform issue. Moffett came to believe that alcohol caused much evil in society. He joined a Prohibition society, printed a local Prohibition broad sheet, and traveled the region giving speeches against "the demon rum."

On August 23, 1889, Moffett gave a talk in Chatham against liquor in which he stated, "I would rather have good Negro rule than the rule of the alcoholic devil." He meant to compare the evils of liquor to that of "Negro rule."

Danville Democrats didn't take it that way. Within days the Danville *Times* printed an editorial asking Moffett to explain his speech: "Good Negro rule! Where did you get such an idea? Who

---

98 Eric Foner, *Reconstruction* (New York: Harper & Row, 1988), pp.IX-XX

had ever heard of, or even dreamed of such a thing? We are sorry to hear such an expression coming from such a respectable source, just on the eve of a great battle for the supremacy of the white race." The paper referred to the Virginia gubernatorial race in the last comment.

The *Danville Register* denounced Moffett's "modern Utopia where good Negroes hold the sway of government and white men and white women are peaceful and happy under the dark regime…the people of Danville and North Danville, who have tasted the bitter fruits of Negro rule, fear it and fight it as they do small pox, yellow fever, or leprosy." The paper had no doubt that Moffett "will set himself right before the people."

Moffett wrote a reply against what he saw as "hot headed Democrats mad because I chose to set whisky worse than the Negro." Moffett dismissed the *Times* "as a paper liberally supported by the liquor men of Danville." He continued, "I would rather be governed by a good Negro than by a drunken white man. Everybody will see, however, who reads the piece calmly that I am right," or so he thought.

The *Times* called his reply "worse and worse" and told Moffett to get back in "his sphere" and out of "ours." The paper then styled Moffett as the "champion of good Negro rule" and accused him of supporting Mahone, who was running as a Republican that year. It then warned Moffett "woe be unto you" if the Democrats were to lose.

Through his broadsheet, the *Anti-Liquor*, Moffett began to oppose Democratic candidates who didn't live up to his moral standards. He drew wrath by preaching a sermon in which he announced that he felt compelled to speak out against any party that supported liquor. He would not allow "the RACE PROBLEM" to stop him. "I want to say right here that I have as much horror as anyone of a government ruled by semi-civilized, superstitious, improvident, uneducated, often brutal, recently set of free slaves," he assured, but he believed that "our plan for controlling the colored man" is "contrary to God's plan…founded on hate, and on corruption and dishonesty at the ballot box."

J.T. Clark, a local Democrat and attorney, argued with Moffett in the papers over his views. Clark circulated a petition "to buy a lot and build a house for a Negro by Moffett's home." During a Prohibition rally a man came out of the crowd, went up to Moffett, placed a pistol up against his chest and pulled the trigger. It misfired and the man ran off.

The day after the next election Moffett and Clark got into an argument in the street. Clark pulled a gun out and shot Moffett. Local Democrats had honored Clark the night before as the man who "exposed Moffett."

Moffett died twenty-eight hours after the shooting and Clark went on trial in Judge Aiken's courtroom for murder. A team of four lawyers from Danville's most prestigious law firms defended Clark. The fact that he could not afford their fees has caused one researcher of the incident to speculate that Democrats paid them.

The jury was split. On their first informal vote some of them voted for acquittal while others voted for first-degree murder. Eventually they ended up with five voting for second-degree murder and seven for manslaughter. After the jury gave Clark the compromise verdict of manslaughter, Judge Aiken gave him a reduced sentence of five years in prison.

Moffett joined the men shot down during the Danville riot as a sacrifice to the altar of white supremacy and Democratic rule.[99]

As for William Sims, he was warned never to return to Chatham and moved to Washington D.C. where he served as a bookkeeper in the Senate printing room. He then became a consul for the State Department in Panama, where he died in 1891 due to cerebral meningitis. In the aftermath of the riot he wrote a friend, "I long to see the day when truth and justice, freedom of thought, and speech, and equality of all men under the law will triumph over race prejudice, partisan hate, and proscription."[100]

---

99 Richard Hamm, *Murder, Honor, and Law: Four Virginia Homicides from Reconstruction to the Great Depression* (Charlottesville: University of Virginia Press, 2003), pp.65-96.
100 *New York Times*, December, 9, 1888; www.victorianvilla.com/sims-mitchell/history/sims_william/index.htm

CHAPTER TWO: My Brother's Keeper: *The Rise of Dan River Mills and the Good Government Club*

In the decade following the Danville riot, the men who held city council positions were for the most part small businessmen. In the 1880s, forty-four out of fifty-four city council members were small proprietors or partners in small businesses, most of which were involved in trading tobacco, tobacco manufacturing, or wholesale merchandising. To a large extent this was a reflection of their importance to the Danville economy.[101]

Until the end of the Civil War slaves were used as laborers in Danville's tobacco factories, which produced plugs of tobacco used for chewing or smoking. Once the war ended, the former slaves remained in the factories as free laborers and received wages for their work. William Sutherlin, who had the largest tobacco factory in Danville, hired approximately a hundred such workers. He didn't believe that the abolition of slavery caused his business any harm. To the Virginia State Agricultural Society, he argued that slavery's end would only injure a "parasitic minority" of plantation owners while those with a vigorous spirit of entrepreneurship would prevail and become Virginia's new class of wealth and leadership.[102]

---

101 William Mainwaring, *Community in Danville, Virginia, 188-1963* (Ph.D. dissertation: University of North Carolina at Chapel Hill, 1988), pp. 105-106.

102 Jeffrey Kerr-Ritchie, *Freedpeople in the Tobacco South* (Chapel Hill: The University of North Carolina Press, 1999), p. 114; Barbara Bennett, *William T. Sutherlin and the Danville Tobacco Industry* (MA. Thesis, The University of North Carolina at Greensboro, 1974), p. 25.

The fortunes of Danville rose and fell with the tobacco market. After the Civil War tobacco sales boomed. The city's population rose from 3,700 in 1860 to 7,500 by 1880, making it one of the largest cities in between Baltimore and Atlanta. In fact, there was no larger city within one hundred miles of Danville. Charlotte had a population of 7,100 while Greensboro lagged behind with a population of 2,100. However, in the late 1880s and 1890s the tobacco industry underwent enormous changes, which undermined the small businessmen of Danville.[103]

The evolution of the tobacco industry paralleled the evolution of the national economy after the Civil War. From the end of the Civil War to the turn of the century the United States went through an industrial and financial revolution that changed the entire nation. Railroads multiplied throughout the country, bringing counties closer together and creating a national market. Factories displaced small manufacturers as national brands appeared on the shelves of country stores. The growth of large-scale businesses meant the spread of corporations and trusts to manage them. "Robber barons" such as Daniel Drew, John Rockefeller, Jay Cooke, and J. P. Morgan built fortunes through the hook and crook of monopolies and stock manipulation to yield an unprecedented influence over national affairs. As a result Danville's sole proprietors eventually found themselves besieged by national tobacco trusts and railroad combinations.

Across the Virginia/North Carolina border in Durham, James Buchanan Duke began to mass produce cigarettes with the James Bonsack continuous-process cigarette machine. Through mass production and advertising, he created the country's first national brand of cigarettes and through rebates, corporate espionage, and market control he undercut and bought out his competitors. By 1890 Duke forced four of his largest competitors to merge into his American Tobacco Company trust. Smaller companies went bankrupt. In North Carolina the number of tobacco factories fell

---

103   Mainwaring, pp. 102-104.

from 253 in 1894 to thirty-three in 1914, one-eighth the number that had existed a mere two decades earlier.[104]

At the same time, the price of tobacco dropped from thirteen cents a pound in 1883 to eight cents a pound by 1892, putting pressure on tobacco merchants and warehouse owners, who feared that the American Tobacco Company would drive prices even lower. In 1896 a group of Danville manufacturers formed the Southern Manufacturers Association to lobby against the trust, but by the end of the nineteenth century almost all of Danville's tobacco factories had closed their doors.

Danville's businessmen found their profits not just under attack from tobacco trusts, but also from J. P. Morgan's Southern Railway combination. The Southern Railway purchased all of the rail lines that passed through Danville. Merchants believed that it used the power of monopoly to charge high rates. The *Danville Register* called it an "anaconda system that is squeezing the life out of our people." Danville's politicians fought, with little success, to pass legislation to regulate rail rates.

Danville's sole proprietors, who prided themselves on being economically and politically independent, took measures to protect what they saw as the public interest against the power of large corporations and combinations outside of town. In 1893 voters in Pittsylvania County voted for Populist Party candidates, who sought to regulate corporations and protect small farmers, and supported William Jennings Bryan's run for president in 1896. A few years earlier, Danville's city council chose to build its own municipally owned electric power plant rather than allow a private corporation to have a monopoly over local power rates.[105]

Despite the widespread hostility toward large companies at the time, Danville soon became home to the largest textile corporation in the world. At first the city council and small business-

---

104 C. Van Woodward, *Origins of the New South, 1877-1913* (USA: Louisiana State University Press, 1951), pp. 308-309; Alfred D. Chandler, Jr., *The Visible Hand* (USA: Belknap, 1977), pp. 382-385.

105 Mainwaring, pp. 111, 116, 118-121.

men looked at the mill warily, but within a few decades the mill changed the city's demographics and would have its own influence over city politics and the Danville community. Small entrepreneurs would find themselves displaced from politics as the mill and its allies gained more and more influence over Danville's affairs.

William Sutherlin did not live to see these changes take place. He died in 1893, just as tobacco's importance in Danville began to wane. In many ways he was the archetypical Danville business-man of the nineteenth century. With his business dependent on the tobacco trade, he became a leader of the local Grange, which brought local tobacco farmers and merchants together so that they could maintain stable prices. They saw monopolistic railroads and the American Tobacco Company as their main nemeses. Sutherlin organized the Border Grange Bank of Danville, which provided capital and credit to area farmers, and remained active in Grange activities until his death. If Sutherlin was representative of his time, then Robert Addison Schoolfield typified the next phase of Danville's history.[106]

The Life of Robert Addison Schoolfield

R. A. Schoolfield was born forty-five miles west of Danville in Henry County to Reverend William Schoolfield and his wife Sarah in 1853. Reverend Schoolfield died two years later. "My father was an intermit Methodist preacher when a young man," his son later recalled, adding that after his father married he gave "up his connection as a traveling preacher, a few years later he located in Henry Country, Virginia, at which time he went into the mer-cantile business and continued the same the balance of his life. As a local preacher he continued to preach in neighborhoods up to the time of his death." He left his wife with eight children, Robert Schoolfield being the youngest.

R. A. Schoolfield grew up with his two older brothers, William and James. The rest of his siblings had either married or left home.

---

106 Bennett, pp. 63-65.

During the Civil War, the three brothers ran the small Schoolfield farm. As soon as Schoolfield matured sufficiently enough he tended the fields, cut firewood, and fed livestock. His mother hauled water, wove, and took up sewing chores.[107]

Despite the hard work, Schoolfield had a playful childhood. He derived great enjoyment from hunting with his dog. Fifty years later he wrote:

> When I was a little boy living at our old home, I would get the long rifle, about as tall as or taller than I was long and put it on my shoulder and walk out and call Spot, and when I would say "come on little doggy" he would prance around and wag his tail and seem perfectly delighted to go hunting for some squirrels. When he barked I would go to the tree where he was and put on my old rifle by the side of a tree and point it at the squirrel that Spot had found. When I would shoot and the squirrel would fall, Spot would run and pick it up in his mouth and shake it until it was dead. Sometimes the squirrel would squeal and then again sometimes the squirrel would bite Spot and he would squeal. I would take the squirrel from him and run a little stick through its foot, put my gun on my shoulder, taking the little squirrels in my hand and we would go off hunting for another.[108]

Although most of his older siblings had left home to start new families, the duties of the farm and the hardship of the Civil War left Schoolfield with only a rudimentary education. Local schools shut down during the war after the lion's share of money and resources had been diverted to the Confederate army. With the

---

107 Eugene King, Robert Addison Schoolfield: *A Biographical History of the Leader of Danville, Virginia's Textile Mills during their first Fifty Years* (Richmond: William Byrd Press, 1979), pp. 4, 9.

108 Robert Addison Schoolfield Papers, 1855-1973, Accession #10325, University of Virginia Library, Charlottesville, Virginia.

Bible and McGuffey Readers, though, his mother gave him lessons in reading, writing, and arithmetic.

Once R. A. Schoolfield reached the age of sixteen in 1869, he took his first job away from home as a clerk in a nearby country store. Six months later he left to work in a general store purchased by his brother John. "In both stores I did general work as well as sell goods. I remained with my brother in this capacity for about six years at which time I was taken as a partner and remained in business with him as J. H. Schoolfield and Brother for four years. During this time I was also partner for the year with a brother-in-law, firm name was Jas. P. France & Co., in the manufacturer of tobacco," he wrote.

While Schoolfield worked with his brother, he occasionally had to take trips a few times a year to purchase supplies for the store. Twice a year R. A. went to Richmond. One trip he took to Reidsville, North Carolina, he found worthy enough to record for posterity. He paid $1 to take a train home from Reidsville to Danville, then stayed overnight and boarded a train for Richmond. Schoolfield wrote that while on the train he "met with the prettiest girl I ever saw, would give anything in the world to be acquainted to talk to her a little sometimes. Anyway bought papers and loaned them to her and she thanked me so nicely it completely won my heart. She got off at Meherrin 1st station in Amelia and walked off as pretty and gracefully as could possibly be. She had gotten on the train at Barksdale, and I had a disappealing ride after she left." Schoolfield never saw her again.[109]

Schoolfield married Annie France of Asheville, North Carolina, in 1885. Both grew up in Henry County and had three brothers and sisters who intermarried, a common occurrence at the time. R. A. and Annie had three children, two of whom died in early childhood. Annie France died only twelve years after their marriage. Two years later Schoolfield remarried.

Schoolfield had a quiet personal life and piously disdained parties, card playing, dancing, drinking, and even plays. Most of his social activities revolved around his church where he served as

---

109 King, pp. 10-16.

a steward and trustee. Many of his church-related friends visited his home and over the years he opened it to "every preacher that ever passed through town." Reverend Rawling, Schoolfield's pastor, remembered him as being "modest, retiring, rarely speaking in public and then only when forced, but in everything that was going on in the Church, albeit, behind the scenes, was not only a well-wisher, but a very energetic and powerful promoter of anything that was forward-looking and large."[110]

Schoolfield attended the Main Street Methodist Church in Danville. He would later remember that period in his life:

> Forty years ago I was a small potato, but united myself with the Main Street Church and Sunday school and have been a member ever since. I joined Judge Peatross's class on the first Sunday in January, 1883. My recollection is that I attended Sunday school every Sunday that year, including the 4th day of November, the day after the riot Saturday afternoon, after having been up with others patrolling the streets the night before. There were very few people present, though, that morning. For my faithful attendance that year I was presented, at Christmas entertainment, a ten cent jumping jack.[111]

Robert Schoolfield and the Founding of Dan River Mills

Robert Schoolfield's older brother James became the first Schoolfield to live in Danville, having moved to the town in 1873 to open up a hardware store named Schoolfield, Vass, and Company. The store had 4,300 square feet upon which it sold stoves, paints, oils, hardware, farming implements, and machinery. John Schoolfield spent most of his time as a traveling preacher and worked in the store only part time. His brother-in-law, H. F. Vass, handled most of the business.

---

110 Ibid., pp.73-87.
111 Robert Addison Schoolfield papers.

A few years after John Schoolfield moved to Danville, his brothers Robert and James, who continued to run their country store in Henry County, contracted neuralgia, a disorder of the facial nerves. James got over his illness in just a few months, but Robert's condition persisted for over a year. During this time R. A. Schoolfield took a trip to Columbus, Georgia, to rest and recover.

While he stayed in Columbus, he visited a successful textile plant, the Eagle and Phoenix Mills. The factory had been built after the Civil War and recently underwent a tremendous expansion. By the time of Schoolfield's visit they had an impressive twenty-five thousand spindles and a market capitalization of one million dollars. The company paid dividends of 18 percent a share and had a stock price that had been rapidly appreciating.[112]

Similar plants had sprung up throughout the South after the Civil War with more and more being constructed as the region approached the twentieth century. In 1880 forty-five mills existed in the South. By 1890, that number grew to 119 and in 1900 there were 357 mills in the South. Textile factories were the first large-scale industrial plants in the South.[113]

This followed the pattern of other nations and regions in their earliest stages of industrialization. Textile plants served as the first large-scale manufacturing factories in Great Britain, New England, Japan, India, and more recently in the third-world nations of today. The reason for this is that the plants are easy to transport, require simple machinery, and have low start-up costs. At the time Southern textile workers also earned wages that averaged 30 to 50 percent lower than their New England counterparts, a fact that made their products more competitive and encouraged investors to pool their resources into building more and more textile mills in the region.[114]

---

112 King, pp. 20,29.
113 Woodward, p. 135.
114 Douglas Flamming, *Creating the Modern South: Millhands and Managers in Dalton, Georgia, 1884-1984* (Chapel Hill: University of North Carolina Press, 1992), pp. 24-25; Gavin Wright, *Old South, New South* (Baton Rouge: Louisiana State University Press, 1986), p. 130.

Robert Schoolfield saw this economic revolution in the South and decided that Danville, with the Dan River as a source of electric power, would be an attractive place to build a plant. In the time period surrounding the Danville riot, Democrats in Danville were also interested in developing industry. "Politics were very lively...parties in developing water power here were anxious to bring white labor here to break the Negro rule," Schoolfield wrote. "I never took a very active part in politics," he continued, "but on account of the conditions prevailing at the time, of course I was very interested and at times attended some of the ward meetings."

R.A. Schoolfield's brother James brought together the people who made his dream a reality. In 1882, a group of six men met in James Schoolfield's home and founded the Riverside Cotton Mills. They included Robert, James, and John Schoolfield as well as B. F. Jefferson, Dr. H.W. Cole, and Thomas Fitzgerald. Fitzgerald, a building contractor, built the mills, and Jefferson, who owned a lumber mill, provided the wood. After a few years Cole sold his stock back to the other founders and turned a quick profit for his involvement.

By 1894, the company had six mills in operation and was fast becoming one of the largest textile operations in the South. "The growth of this company far exceeded anyone's dreams," Robert Schoolfield wrote. "With our reputation and the quality of our cloth we were well and favorably known to the trade throughout the country and as customers we had the names on our books of practically all of the best concerns of the United States."

Fueled by profits, the mill founders formed a subsidiary company that operated power generators along the Dan River. In 1909, they combined the two companies to form the Riverside and Dan River Cotton Mills, a name that would remain until 1946 when the corporation became known as Dan River Mills, Incorporated. By the mid 1980s the company once again changed its name to the simplified Dan River, Incorporated.[115]

---

115 Robert Addison Schoolfield papers.

The founders made Fitzgerald the company's first president and appointed Robert Schoolfield to be its secretary, treasurer, and general manager. With those titles in hand, Schoolfield took over most of Dan River's administrative duties, but he had one problem. As he later recalled, "I knew nothing of the cotton mill business and neither did any of our directors."

Schoolfield took a trip back down to Columbus, Georgia, and searched for someone familiar with the textile business who could serve as superintendent. "I got in touch with Mr. S. I. Roberts, who was subsequently employed for that position," Schoolfield wrote. "We were fortunate in making the selection we did. After talking with him, we decided to make an entirely different class of goods from that previously contemplated, and that change was a most fortunate one." A year later George Robertson also left Georgia to become the company's overseer of weaving.[116]

Schoolfield traveled up to Biddeford, Maine, and bought the machinery used to operate Dan River's first plant. Production started with a hundred looms and 2,200 spindles. Twenty years later Dan River operated seven separate mills in Danville with a total of 2,771 looms and 66,650 spindles. The spectacular growth of the company brought thousands of people to Danville, causing the number of people living in the city between 1883 and 1900 to grow from 3,500 to 16,500.[117]

Most of the people who initially came to work in the mills were farmers. Falling produce prices made farming difficult and many families found themselves forced to find another way to earn a living. Mill recruiters and posters appeared in the Virginia mountains, enticing them to leave the farm for "public" work. Families who heeded their call often wrote back to relatives to tell them to join them. One such letter reads:

---

116 Ibid; Robert Sidney Smith, *Mill on the Dan* (North Carolina: Duke University Press, 1960), p.15.
117 King, pp.42, 64; Danville Chamber of Commerce, *Danville Virginia: An Industrial Survey*, 1940.

Dear Uncle Willie,

This is sure different from being tenants on the tobacco farm in Sutherlin. After we sold our crop, we moved here and now I can go to school. Since I never got to go very much to school I am far behind for my age and size, Miss Brimmer says. She is my teacher. But she says that she will help me catch up. I stay after school and work during the recess too so I can be good at ciphering and reading...Mama is working in the Schoolfield mill and grandma keeps the house. Dad had gone to the country to stay with his sister because his health is not too good since he had typhoid fever some time back. But we are managing our four-room house. It is plenty big enough for all five of us children and mama and grandma. Our street is on a hill not far from the rail tracks.

We miss you but you were right. They want people with sizeable families to come. You and Aunt Sallie might not qualify you just being two of you.

Yours truly,
Oscar, your nephew

While Oscar reveled in his life and his family's success in moving from farm to factory, it is clear that not every such economy-forced transition was as successful. Mary Collins wrote a bitter contrast to Oscar's joyous missive:

Dear Sister Mattie,

A very terrible thing has happened. Last week a train struck Lloyd at the railroad crossing near our home here on Selma Ave and he died instantly. You know he was a little hard of hearing all his life but we don't really know why he didn't see or hear the train coming.

We buried him in the Green Street Cemetery in Danville. I will never get over this as long as I live. I may move away from here as soon as I can find another job.

They say there are job openings in the Leaksville mills.
This place is more than I can bear now.

I hope you family is fine. Granny sends her love. We
wanted to let you know of our great sorrow.

Love, Mary Collins[118]

Families were encouraged to transplant their family-farm
work unit into the factory by mill managers across the South.
Most of the people who worked in Southern mills between 1880
and 1900 were between the ages of sixteen and twenty-four, with
more than twice as many females as males. Young girls, who ma-
ture faster than boys and have small and nimble fingers, were giv-
en the more numerous spinners jobs. In 1896 President Fitzgerald
reported that "perhaps 700" children worked in the mills. In 1950
the company's retirement rolls listed Alice Thompson as having
begun her employment at Dan River in 1888 at the age of eleven.
The records also show that William Morgan entered the mill in
the same year a few months before his ninth birthday.[119]

Dan River had a hard time keeping its first employees, many of
whom had trouble adjusting to factory life. According to Robert
Schoolfield, "We had to import or teach the operators how to
run the machinery. The imported labor was, as a whole, migratory
and unsatisfactory." He blamed some of these problems on weak
moral fiber.

In order to improve the character of his employees and make
them more efficient, Schoolfield told Superintendent S. I. Roberts
to encourage the workers to attend church and to discourage
them from drinking alcohol. However, Schoolfield recalled, "We
were placed at a disadvantage on account of the unfriendly attitude of a very large number of Danville citizens because our
position on alcohol conflicted with their mercenary interests."[120]

---

118 Nell Collins Thompson, *Echoes from the Mills* (Roanoke: Toler Printing Company,
      1984), p.21.

119 Wright, pp.138-140; Smith, p.48.

120 Robert Addison Schoolfield papers; Smith, p.49.

One day Schoolfield got into an altercation over the issue. He recounted the episode:

> I was riding with Mr. Roberts, our Superintendent, in his buggy going to the Long Mill. Mr. Roberts was very much disliked by the whiskey people on account of his constant fight against the use of it. After crossing the bridge and starting toward the mill I felt a jar to the buggy and saw a man close by that hit it with a stick. He had previously had some quarrel with Mr. Roberts that I knew nothing about. Mr. Roberts usually carried a cane with him. So I picked up the cane, got out of the buggy, and went toward this man, who quickly got out of the way and ran into a bar room close by. I followed him as far as the door, but did not go further. A policeman close by, who was more or less in sympathy with the whiskey people, was kind enough to have me summoned to court for assault.[121]

Dan River Mills and the Danville Community

Alcohol is only one issue that sparked anger toward the mill. Schoolfield's company often found itself standing alone against the rest of Danville's business community. After "having tried working in projects with the Chamber of Commerce and with other citizens, I concluded that more could be accomplished through individual efforts," Schoolfield wrote. That attitude often created conflict between Schoolfield and the town's small merchants and remaining tobacco businessmen.[122]

Danville's smaller businessmen had come to believe that J. P. Morgan's Southern Railway Company, which had bought all of the railroads that passed through Danville, used the power of monopoly to charge unfair rates. In 1899 the city of Danville filed a suit with the Interstate Commerce Commission (ICC) against the company. Although the commission ruled in the city's favor, a

121 Robert Addison Schoolfield papers.
122 Ibid.

federal court overturned its decision. Danville's merchants saw another opportunity to fight the Southern Railway when the U.S. Senate held hearings on strengthening the powers of the ICC. The businessmen hoped that the Senate would give the ICC the authority to set rates independently of the federal courts.

Danville sent a delegation led by Judge A. M. Aiken and attorney Eugene Withers to the Senate. After delivering a petition in favor of more regulation, Judge Aiken spoke, insisting that the Southern Railway was deliberately trying to ruin Danville by charging high freight rates in revenge for the city's previous suits against the company. A few days later, however, an unofficial delegation from Danville appeared before the Senate, repudiated Aiken, and said that Morgan's railroad had "done a great deal for Danville."

This delegation, whose members presented themselves as a flour miller, a furniture dealer, a mill executive, and a banker, created quite a stir back in Danville. The city's official delegation denied that the second delegation spoke for the city. According to the *Danville Register*, "No incident has happened in this city for many years that has caused such a commotion."

It turned out that three of the four men in the second delegation were directors of Dan River Mills. Robert Schoolfield had joined the delegation and so had James Pritchett, who claimed to be a "wealthy miller." Pritchett operated a flour mill that was owned by the textile company. Only one of the men, William Boatwright, a wholesale furniture dealer, had no direct connection to Dan River Mills.

Ray Baker, a reporter for the *Danville Register*, discovered that Dan River Mills and the furniture company, because they dealt in bulk goods, were being charged lower rates by the Southern Railroad than the smaller businessmen in town. Baker concluded that 95 percent of Danville's population suffered as a result of the railroad monopoly. As evidence he pointed to abandoned and dilapidated tobacco warehouses that filled the city's business district and a sharp drop in the number of wholesale merchants in the city. This wasn't the only case that made the mill seem like a villain in the eyes of the rest of the Danville business and civic communities.[123]

Immediately after Dan River Mills was founded, the city of Danville granted it a ten-year tax exemption. In 1892, the company received another ten-year tax exemption, but found that it had to beg for it. The textile company owned eleven out of twelve power generators along the Dan River. The city leased the remaining generator from a third party. In 1893, Dan River Mills proposed building another factory along the river. Schoolfield approached the city about selling or sharing its electrical power in order to operate the new factory. The city council, however, "backed by public sentiment," placed what Schoolfield thought was an "exorbitant price" on the power.

Schoolfield decided to forget about the city council and persuaded the board of directors of Dan River Mills to build its new facilities across the river and north of the city. The company's management continued to view the city's power generator as a "standing menace" and bought it once the city's lease expired. The textile company then owned a monopoly on the power and water plants on the Dan River. When the city engineer, C. A. Ballou, asked the company for additional water for a municipal power plant, the company refused. The city then turned to a separate steam generating plant to prevent dependence on the mill company.

In 1902 the company began construction of what would become the giant Schoolfield mill complex, which, in the words of the mill executives, was built "out of reach of city officials, who we fear from past experience, will continue to harass us." Months later city officials made an attempt to extend Danville's city limits to include the new mill properties. George Cabell, who by then served in the Virginia House of Delegates, introduced a bill to annex the property. However, two state senators intervened and kept the bill from coming out of committee. Both of them happened to own stock in Dan River Mills.[124]

---

123 Mainwaring, pp. 144-146.
124 Ibid., pp. 125-132, 139-142.

During its first twenty years of operation Dan River Mills consistently acted in a manner that put its interests ahead of Danville's small businessmen and entrepreneurs. This pattern won it few friends, but created many enemies. No event made this clearer than a strike by its workers in 1901, a time in which the company found itself at odds with the entire city.

A Ten-Hour Day

In 1889 employees at Dan River Mills worked twelve hours a day, six days a week, and earned an average of eighty-eight cents a day. All employees over fourteen worked a standard twelve-hour day until the Virginia legislature passed a bill that made it illegal for children under fourteen to work more than ten hours a day. The long hours and low wages were standard throughout the Southern textile mill industry.[125]

One worker remarked, "Twelve hours a day is too long for anyone to work in a mill." Chester Copeland, who worked in a mill in North Carolina, called it a "robot life." Copeland left mill work and returned to farming. "Robot-ing is my word for it," he said, "in the mill you do the same thing over and over again, just like on a treadmill. There's always something exciting and changing in nature. It's never a boring job. There's some dirty jobs in farming, but there's nothing you get more pleasure out of than planting, growing, and then harvesting." Mill worker John Wesley Snipes said, "I never had no use for a cotton mill. Look at it run twelve hours a day, and the same old thing in the morning, and the same old thing next morning. I didn't like it at all, but I had to do it. I had to make bread and butter."[126]

Workers at Dan River Mills began petitioning management for a ten-hour working day. The company executives reported "some agitation going on among some of the Mill operatives, be-

---

125 Smith, pp.45-47.
126 Jacquelyn Hall, James Leloudis, Robert Korstad, Mary Murphy, Lu Ann Jones, and Christopher Daly, *Like A Family: The Making of a Southern Cotton Mill World* (Chapel Hill: University of North Carolina Press, 1987), pp. 54, 77.

ing incited by one of the Attorneys of the town, who, it seems has political aspirations." At first Robert Schoolfield blamed the discontent on George Cabell, but came to realize that the workers were, in fact, organizing on their own.

Schoolfield told the board of directors that the workers' goals "are very reaching and their object is to control or dictate to management." Without recognizing the union or making any statement about public opinion, the company reduced the working day to eleven hours in January of 1900. The following October it lowered the working day by another hour, although the company announced that it would return to an eleven-hour daily schedule in April.

As April approached the union movement grew stronger. The American Federation of Labor, seeing Dan River Mills as "the focal point for the entering of the wedge against the injustice and wrong of child labor and long hours in the South," came to Danville to represent and assist its textile workers. Samuel Gompers, president of the AFL and one of the most prominent labor leaders in the United States at the time, came to negotiate personally with the company.

Two days before Dan River was scheduled to return to an eleven-hour day, Gompers met for two hours with Schoolfield and several mill executives. Schoolfield told Gompers that Dan River paid higher wages than textile plants in Greensboro and other parts of the South. He then said that the union "really had no grievance, but a few hot-heads had started something which they were not in a position to finish."

After it became clear that there would be no real negotiations, Gompers left. In the evening he addressed a packed crowd of over one thousand workers and supporters in Danville. Mayor Harry Wooding opened the meeting by giving a speech which "eulogized" the labor leader. Gompers then spoke, observing, "The cotton mill operatives of Danville have had a taste of freedom, and now realized that they needed time to improve themselves, to learn, to love, to breathe...A citizenship based on twelve hours work per day was a poor citizenship. They had no time to inform themselves on issues of government and politics and become valuable self-thinking, reading, and reasoning citizens." Gompers said that he did not like strikes, but there is "value of striking power when arbitration fails." After he finished, the assembly of workers signed a resolution to go on strike if Dan River Mills moved back to an eleven-hour day on April 1, 1901.[127]

After receiving the workers' petition, the company's management convened and decided to ignore their demands. According to Robert Schoolfield, "Conditions were such that it looked as if we either had to control our own property or let the labor unions do it for us." Despite the company's firm stance, the strikers had the support of the rest of the Danville community. A week after the strike began, a delegation of ten local clergymen, including those from the more upper-class First Baptist and Episcopal churches, tried to meet with Schoolfield and the other mill directors in order to "seek a Christian settlement to our differences,"[128] but were turned away.

Eventually the strike crumbled in the face of Dan River Mill's stone resistance. As time passed, workers trickled back to their jobs and by the middle of the summer nothing remained of the strike or the union. Nonetheless, in the spring of 1903 the mill switched back to a ten-hour day on Schoolfield's recommendation. In December of that year the board of directors complained about the loss of production due to a shortened workday, but thought it would be "impractical" to go back to an eleven-hour day.[129]

Although Dan River Mills won the strike, they did so without the support of the rest of the Danville community. Among the union leaders, even "the most disreputable had the sympathy and support of our so-called best citizens," Schoolfield complained. He also found himself annoyed with "sensational"

127 Smith, pp. 51-52.
128 Robert Addison Schoolfield papers, Smith, p. 53.
129 Smith, p. 100.

local newspaper stories, which opposed his company, and local merchants, "who began to fall over their heads" in support of AFL labor leaders. The strike is but another example of the precarious position Dan River Mills held in Danville during its formative years.[130]

Schoolfield's Village

Even though Dan River Mills defeated the union, the company still had trouble with its labor force. As the company grew, it had problems finding enough employees to man the machinery and keep them at work. Labor turnover and inefficiency became a constant irritant to Robert Schoolfield. "Since the open weather," Schoolfield complained in May, 1906, "we have had quite a number of people leave us for outdoor work on railroad and other construction work." He had hoped that by the fall these people would return, but once the leaves turned colors, he complained to the board of directors that "we have been at our wits' end to know what is the best thing to do" about scarce labor.

The company's employees were not unaware of its problems. "On account of the shortage of labor supply," Schoolfield wrote, "we are taken advantage of by people who only seem to want work just days enough to enable them to live. In other words, if they can get by working three days a week, they are disposed to drink, loaf, or rest the balance of the time." In a report to the directors of Dan River Mills, Schoolfield blamed the "unprecedented shortage of labor" on the "re-opening of saloons in our city" which caused "the demoralization among our operatives on account of whiskey drinking and drunkenness."

In order to attract and keep more workers, R. A. Schoolfield and the board of directors decided to build a mill village outside of the Danville city limits next to the Schoolfield plant. The village and the area around the plant became known simply as Schoolfield. As H. R. Fitzgerald, the son of T. B. Fitzgerald, one of the founders

---

130 Robert Addison Schoolfield papers.

of the mill, recalled, "We had about digested the supply [of labor] in our immediate community, so that it became necessary to develop the village of Schoolfield." The company built its first ten four-room houses on Park Avenue a few hundred yards away from the factory in 1903. Six years later the village consisted of 445 houses. Each house had essentially the same design, materials, and color. Standard outhouses, each of which was built fifty paces from the rear door of each home, accentuated the monotony of row upon row of houses.

The construction of the mill village was only one of the company's services for its workers. After noting that "our village has been visited with epidemics, resulting in a large amount of sickness and a number of deaths," Schoolfield authorized the building of a hospital. A nursery and kindergarten followed. Soon the company added a bowling alley, pool room, motion picture theater, and a hall which prohibited the use of "spirituous or malt liquors," card playing, or dancing.[131]

Mill villages existed throughout the South wherever there were textile plants. So did company baseball teams, recreational services, and company stores. To manage all of these programs the mill hired Hattie Hylton as superintendent of welfare. It also funded its own fire and police departments. In effect Schoolfield operated as a town owned by a private company. All life in Schoolfield revolved around Dan River Mills. Entertainment and recreation outside of the factory floor still involved the company. Most of the workers were delivered by a company doctor when born, attended a school funded by the company, spent the rest of their lives working for it, and were given eulogies by preachers whose churches received money from the company when they died.[132]

Labor historians have since called this paternalism, describing these non-wage benefits as an attempt to build a corporate culture which regulated the living environment of workers. The management of Dan River Mills called it "welfare work." Although

---

131 Smith, pp. 105-109.
132 Thompson, p. 30.

the aim of Schoolfield village was to create a more efficient work-force, the directors believed that their programs uplifted their workers, whom they often saw as primitives before they came to the mill.

Writing to one mill executive, H. R. Fitzgerald, said, "I would not now attempt to describe the conditions that existed among virtually all of these families [from the mountain districts of Virginia and the Carolinas] in their state of run-down poverty and ignorance, and eking out a precarious existence on mountain farms. Some of the worst cases of disease and a long chain of evils and vices that had grown in their methods of living were enough to shock the sensibilities of anyone who loves humanity." In a similar vein, Schoolfield wrote, "Many of the people when they first come here seem to have acquired little in the art of living." In reality the village accompanied every benefit it gave its workers with the cost of conformity.[133]

The mill celebrated the village and the community once a year in the "Schoolfield Patriotic Pageant," a march through the village, which ended with music and celebration. The line of the march included the Red Cross, Garden Boys, Junior ROTC, Mother's Club, Odd Fellows, Red Men, mill departments, and "loyal citizens." The president of the mill led it. The industry journal *Textile World* claimed that the pageant helped to dispel "the lack of dignity probably attached to the work of an operative in a cotton mill. Visualizing the function of such a worker as one of the cleanest and most useful occupations in the industrial world, the company has conscientiously set itself the task of helping the worker to see his job in this light, to acquire self-respect and consequently to engender respect in others."

In 1923 an industry group filmed parts of the pageant and incorporated them into a motion picture called "The Story of Cotton." The group distributed the movie throughout the United States in the belief that "most of the women who now buy the

133 Smith, p. 108; Flamming, p. 121.

products of the mills do not know the conditions under which the products are manufactured." The film's producers sought to show "that these products are not made by cheap labor under sweat shop conditions."[134]

Many workers found the Schoolfield village to be a source of strength and solace. Ray Clifton, who started work as a weaver in the 1920s and later worked as a fireman in Schoolfield, compared it to a family. "Back in the old days," he recalled, "they had the band stand out there next to the YMCA and on pretty, warm summer nights they had a band leader there and we'd go over and sit in the grass, listen to the band play, or either go over to Hylton Hall and promenade up and down the street for the women over at Hylton Hall. Hylton Hall was built for single women, unmarried women come there to work, they didn't have no place to stay."[135]

The mill village physically isolated the workers of Dan River Mills from the rest of Danville. Before the village was built most of the company's textile workers lived in the town. Ballou Park and a railroad track separated the village from the rest of Danville. The town's councilmen no longer campaigned for the votes of mill workers after they moved outside of the city limits. Moreover, since the mill had its own company store and provided most of the necessities of life, including entertainment, its workers didn't need to travel to Danville often.

The growth of Dan River Mills altered the social dynamics of Danville itself. In the nineteenth century a class of small entrepreneurs and small businessmen led the town. When compared to the mill owners and the factory hands, there was not much difference between them and their employees or the tobacco merchants who moved goods throughout region and used Danville as their base. However, as the tobacco trade faltered and large corporations mass produced goods and put small merchants out of business, these men faded away. At the same time, the growth of

---

134 Smith, p.253.
135 Thompson, p.36.

textiles created a new class of middle managers and white-collar employees of the mill that displaced them.

In 1901 the textile company had an office staff of nine people. By 1916 the number of people drawing salaries over $2,000 a year jumped to twenty-four. The number of office secretaries, bookkeepers, and stenographers multiplied even more. Chain stores also opened up in Danville. The men who managed these stores were oriented toward a national market and operated in a corporate flow chart, unlike the small merchants who had existed before them.[136]

This new corporate middle class announced its existence through the formation of the Chamber of Commerce, a Retail Merchants Association, a Young Business Men's Business Club, the Danville Rotary Club, the Kiwanis Club, and the Lions Club. Not to be left behind, the middle-class women of Danville formed the Professional Women's Club and the YWCA. All of these organizations were formed between 1915 and 1922 and set its members apart from the older Mason, Odd Fellows, and Elks clubs, which were more egalitarian.

The women's Wednesday Club and the Danville Golf Club sat on top of the social hierarchy. Founded in 1922, the Danville Golf Club accepted only the city's most elite businessmen and their friends as members. In contrast, the Freemasons, which existed as the most prominent social club during the nineteenth century, accepted people from all elements of white society. [137]

The men who now considered themselves the Danville "elite" were more self-conscious about their position than the George Cabells and William Sutherlins of the nineteenth century. The differences between these men and the classes of people below them, not only in wealth, but also in culture and taste, probably caused this. Also, unlike William Sutherlin, Robert Schoolfield did not know all his employees by name and used intermediaries such as Hattie Hylton and S. I. Roberts to deal with them.

---

136 Mainwaring, pp. 172-174.
137 Mainwaring, pp. 176-177.

By 1910, the elites of Danville saw Dan River Mills and its employees differently than those who lived twenty years before them. The previous small entrepreneurs and businessmen of the town often portrayed the mill as a hostile force. Danville's newspaper writers and preachers criticized the mill and often complained about the company's working conditions. Yet all of this had changed by 1910.

The town's blacks ceased to be citizens after the Danville Riot of 1883 and the voting disenfranchisement created by Virginia's 1902 Constitution. By 1910 most of the town's white textile workers had also stopped voting. Instead of independent citizens, they had become wards of the mill.

The new middle class of Danville often saw the mill workers as below the social status of blacks. Danville's black community had its own middle class of teachers, preachers, and small businessmen. The mill hands had none of this. Their poor living conditions and lack of polish reaffirmed their low status, while the assistance of the "welfare" programs of Dan River Mills confirmed the company's benevolence in their eyes. Often the mill hands were compared to children in need of guidance, dependent on the charity of their social superiors.

According to Julian Meade, a teacher and reporter in Danville, he was told the same story many times:

> Niggers are the happiest people in the South. Don't worry about the hovels many of them live in, don't bother about their hand-to-mouth existence. They're as carefree as larks. That did very well for a philosophy, if you could forget educated Negroes you knew, intelligent men and women who were not happy as larks and never would be. It was the easiest consolation one could find. Even so it was comforting to say the mill workers for the most part did not seem to feel mistreated or oppressed; I thought it was bad for them to live in houses with no bathrooms, and then, a doctor who visited the mill families told me that the ones who had bathrooms in their houses

would put coal and wood in the tubs and did not seem more satisfied than those who still had to go to the back yard.

Such apocryphal stories about the town's textile workers served to explain away their poor living conditions and rationalized the social order that Dan River Mills created much in the same way as the myth of the Danville Riot explained race relations to the whites of Danville and served as a justification for white supremacy.[138]

When teacher and journalist Meade was a child, he remembered going to church and being suddenly jerked out of the pew by his mother during an elderly minister's sermon. He recalled the incident years later:

> Everyone thought she was ill and several Episcopalians followed us into the vestibule to offer assistance. I was frightened. The scene stayed in my mind but I had to grow older by a number of seasons before I could understand mother's explanation of our abrupt departure from the House of God.
>
> "But what did he say that made you so mad, Mother?"
>
> "He counted all our wealth and blessings—and he thanked God for the glory and magnificence of our mills. You can't imagine what the mills were then. Little children were working at night and there were many abuses. I can't see the glory and magnificence too clearly now. So you can imagine how I felt at the time of that sermon.[139]

The Good Government Club

Until the 1920s, vestiges of the old social order remained in Danville politics. In 1908 friends of Dan River Mills placed an

---

138 Julian Meade, *I Live in Virginia* (New York: Longmans, Green & Co., 1935), p.256.
139 Meade, pp.36-37.

anti-saloon law up for referendum. Opponents of the bill linked the textile company to it, attacking its "tyrannical domination over local political affairs." In one advertisement they asked, "Would it not be better for Danville to be an independent city, with varied industries, giving employment to skilled labor that builds up and makes towns? Or would it rather emulate the North Carolina cotton towns and be controlled by a single industry?"

The bill passed, but was struck down two years later. The campaign marked the last time that the power of Dan River Mills would be used as a political issue until the 1920s, and even then, it would be a one-man campaign. No longer would city councilmen campaign with the objective of expanding the city limits to include Schoolfield or run against mill control of politics.[140]

Despite the disappearance of the mill issue, the company did not have complete sway over the town. The structure of Danville's political system prevented Dan River Mills and the emerging middle class from completely controlling the town's politics. Under Virginia's 1902 Constitution, cities and towns were required to have a bicameral government, consisting of a board of alderman and a common council. In turn, six wards divided Danville. Voters cast ballots only for the candidates in their ward. As a result, politicians campaigned to attract the neighborhood vote.

The system made it easier for small businessmen, who had close contact with the voters, to get elected to the city council. It also gave a voice to working people, who were concentrated in the north Danville ward, despite the poll tax and disenfranchisement.

Members of the old middle class dominated the system. Between 1904 and 1918 out of the 135 positions on the council during that period, machinists, mechanics, carpenters, and foremen occupied eleven of them. Grocers and small merchants made up forty of the positions, while accountants, real estate agents,

---

140 Mainwaring, pp. 160-166; *Danville Register,* April 7, 12, 14, 1908.

physicians, and people involved in the tobacco trade made up the rest.[141]

The new elites that made up the membership of the Chamber of Commerce and the Danville Golf Club found this system frustrating. William Gardner is the perfect example. He came to Danville immediately following the turn of the century and became the city's first automobile dealer and then became the vice president of Danville's largest bank. In 1916 Gardner won election as a councilman representing the north Danville ward.

Owing in large part to the tempestuous nature of ward politics in north Danville, council seats in Gardner's ward had constant turnover. No councilman served for more than two terms between 1908 and 1920. Two years after Gardner's election, fourteen candidates, including two Socialists, ran for five council seats. Gardner won re-election and then sought to overturn the ward system.

A proposal to abolish the ward system first officially came from the Young Men's Business Club. A week later the Chamber of Commerce came out in support of the proposal. Within days, a petition for a new charter circulated throughout the town. The two groups then formed the Good Government Club, with William Gardner as its leader, to promote their plan. Also playing prominent roles in the club were Col. A. B. Carrington, the vice president of Dibrell Brothers, a large tobacco firm, Frederick Townes, and several directors and lawyers from Dan River Mills.

The Good Government Club had the objective of replacing the ward system with a mayoral-city council government that would use at-large elections. Instead of campaigning in neighborhoods, city councilmen would have to capture votes throughout the entire city. The number of people on the city council would also drop from thirty to nine. This would have the effect of diluting any remaining working-class voting strength and would make it more difficult for members of the old middle class as well as small entrepreneurs to get elected. At the same time it would

---

141 Mainwaring, pp.182-183.

increase the importance of the backing of the new middle class clubs, the Golf Club, and the Chamber of Commerce in order to get elected.[142]

On April 1, 1920, the Good Government Club organized a mass meeting of supporters. Among its speakers were Malcolm Harris, an attorney at Dan River Mills, tobacconist George Lea, and Democrat Eugene Withers. Lea had been a participant in the Danville Riot thirty-seven years ago. The men portrayed the new charter as a "progressive reform" that would further "the expedition of public business" by reducing the number of city council members.[143]

The Good Government Club made note that most cities in the United States had abolished bicameral governments. It asked in one advertisement, "Is Danville less progressive than other cities in Virginia?" The club also presented itself as a group of disinterested citizens who contrasted themselves with ward politicians who they claimed used dishonest "boss" rule to create graft and corruption.

The club also claimed that businessmen should run the city. City government had become too large to be trusted to mere politicians and needed the guidance of businessmen, they argued. At first glance this may seem like an odd claim, since most of the people who made up the city council were, in fact, businessmen. What was really at issue, however, was what kind of businessmen. Evidently the creators of the Good Government Club did not consider the small neighborhood grocers and merchants to be real businessmen, because they weren't members of the Chamber of Commerce or the Golf Club like they were.

Rhetoric about "ward bosses" and corruption also seems odd at first glance. No scandals marked Danville politics nor did the Good Government Club label any specific councilman as corrupt. The club used such rhetoric to discredit the political power of

---

142 Ibid., pp. 181-189
143 Ibid., pp. 189-190.

working men and the political threat of the north Danville ward, which had Socialist candidates.[144]

Opponents of the Good Government Club attacked its plan as an undemocratic power grab. They organized their own mass meeting in north Danville and placed their own advertisements in the newspapers. Mill worker Clifton Parrot said, "We are all laboring men. Do I understand that the laboring man will not be eligible to this council?" One ad said that the charter amounted to an insult that "the people of some of the wards of the city are incapable of governing themselves."[145]

Other opponents of the charter portrayed the ward system as the epitome of democracy. Reverend J. C. Holland of the Keen Street Baptist Church claimed that at-large elections meant that even if a candidate "received every vote of those who knew him best, a man in the same ward who was not wanted could secure enough votes to land in the council." Opponents also claimed that south Danville, known for its section of mansions on Main Street called "Millionaires Row," would "empty sand-carts coming to north Danville to improve their sections of the city."

Some ads in opposition to the Good Government Club made fun of its members, naming them the "Goo-Goos." They focused on the youth and experience of the Young Men's Business Club, labeling them "the little boys." They claimed that they would not be able to run a centralized government and would make many mistakes. "Having launched an airship corporation and landed in bankruptcy, the ambitious Young Men's Business Club are launching another airship, which some of its facetious critics are dubbing a hot airship," one ad said.[146]

The Good Government Club ignored these charges and continued its campaign. Before the election they placed an ad in the paper, which asserted that Danville "stood on the threshold of a new era." "What will you do? Vote against the change and be

144 Ibid., pp. 182-184.
145 Ibid., pp. 191-192.
146 Ibid, pp. 193-194.

a KNOCKER, or vote for the change and be a BOOSTER," it asked.

The referendum passed by 1,235 votes to 255. Most of the votes against the charter came from the working-class neighborhoods in the city. However, after the poll tax and widespread disenfranchisement there were still enough working class voters to play key roles in the ward system, in which neighborhood voters were crucial, but not enough to swing a city-wide election.[147]

The new charter had the effect of formalizing the changes in the social system and behind-the-scenes political power in Danville. It demolished the few obstacles that stood in the way of the new middle class and the domination by Dan River Mills of the city's politics.

The leaders of the Good Government Club brought a new ideology to Danville. Unlike the old entrepreneurs who held a Jeffersonian philosophy, which honored independent small businessmen and extolled the virtues of town hall democracy, the Good Government Club praised centralized efficiency and rule from above.

In essence they remade Danville's political system in their own image. Most of the members of the Good Government Club and the other business clubs in Danville worked for large businesses or corporations, which were run with bureaucratic structures headed by a few men at the top. The goal of the new charter was to centralize the city government and make it a managerial-type system. The Good Government Club also claimed that only they could understand the big picture and represent the entire interests of the city. They contrasted themselves with the ward system, which they portrayed as being beset with petty parochialism and selfishness. However, unlike the ward politicians, or even figures such as George Cabell and William Sutherlin from the past, they had little direct interaction with people below them in social status. The view from the top had its own limitations.

---

147 Ibid., pp. 196-197.

The new charter diluted what little working-class and small-business power remained in local politics. Thereafter, almost all city councilmen and elected officials would have the backing of groups such as the Chamber of Commerce and the Danville Golf Club. The Good Government Club presented itself as a spokesman for all of Danville, but in reality it represented only a small clique of elites.

After passage of the charter, the power of the Good Government Club seemed to be so unstoppable that interest in politics waned. After it passed, a city council election had to be held. Things were so quiet that the *Danville Register* reported, "There have been no pre-election speeches or in fact anything to indicate that an election is in prospect." Every candidate to the city council that won had been a member of the Good Government Club. That included F. W. Townes, W. E. Gardner, and A. B. Carrington.[148]

Harry Ficklen Battles the Invisible Government

On June 1, 1924, a candidate for the city council spoke to six hundred people packed into the Majestic Theater located in Danville. The man who took the stage, Harry Ficklen, earned a reputation for being a humorous eccentric and "intrepid speaker." People from all over Danville sat in anticipation of what he would say.

At the center of the stage sat a table on top of which lay a white cloth covering an object. A brown satchel rested beneath the table. Ficklen stood alone on the stage and opened up with the line, "Ladies and gentleman and anonymous people not present."

Ficklen apologized for the fact that no prominent people were there to introduce him. He surmised that A. B. Carrington, the Good Government president of the city council, couldn't attend because he had "tobacco plants to stick," while the police chief

---

148 Ibid., p. 198.

was busy with a bootleg raid. Only one man remained who could introduce him, Andy Gump, a famous cartoon character. But even Gump couldn't make it. Stricken with tuberculosis, Gump sent a statement of introduction, which Ficklen held in his hands. Ficklen read out loud Gump's statement, a self-parody of himself:

I now introduce you to a man who has the highest claim to be known as an evangelist, because the evangelist is the only known profession where a past bad record is a feather in a man's cap—a man who is as popular as Raw Head and Bloody Bones in a kindargten and eats 'em raw, especially girls of tender age and school overweight, and cockerels whose tonsils have been removed—a man as opposed to education as a boy going fishing and illiterate as the average member of a school board. A man who looks backward at his pursuers like the bald-headed snipe of the valley, and occasionally shoots and always hits—a man who does not buy oil stock when you offer a cigar and prefers hot tamales to sob-stuff—a reformed man, who despite his imperfections has struck a stride of progress in his plea for "Greater Danville" that makes him look backward at his racing detractors as a grass hopper looks back at a tumble bug in its complacent grasp of its little world and chirps "who is looney now?"

Ficklen then began his speech by stating that he would use Samuel II: Chapter I, Verse 20, as his text. It reads, "Tell it not in gath, publish it not in the streets of Askelon." He then noted that Danville was a good town, but everyone constantly heard the question, "What is the matter with Danville?" He answered by saying that an "invisible government," made up of the directors of Dan River Mills and the members of the Good Government Club and its allies, held the city back. The problem "is the suppression of important truths and its effect on the community." Ficklen argued that Danville was a "whispering city" in which "people will tell things but invariably end by saying don't quote me...It is this which constitutes the invisible government."

Ficklen then turned to attack what he called "hyphenated-Danvillians." This was "the man who lives in Danville, but whose interests lie beyond the corporate limits and who works for the promotion of his alien holdings" in Schoolfield. "The invisible government can't be reached," Ficklen warned, "Its members seek power by using the women folks and religious organizations to gain their ends."

As he explained, "There is an endorsement faction. It usually starts in the council and runs through the civic clubs to the Retail Merchants Association and then to the Chamber of Commerce. Just a few do it in the name of the people when most of them don't know anything about it." Ficklen derided this as "missionary work in high places." As he finished describing "the invisible government" he pulled the cloth off the object on the table to reveal a physical representation of the establishment, a replica of the famous Victor music player trademark: a little white dog listening to his master's voice.

Ficklen then challenged the other city council candidates to prove their independence from the "invisible government" by answering whether or not they favored annexing Schoolfield. Only the annexation of Schoolfield, he argued, would break up the power of the "invisible government," destroy the system of "representation without taxation," and allow Danville to grow.[149]

Harry Ficklen's opposition to Dan River Mills and the Good Government Club was a throwback to an earlier era in which hostility toward the mill company was common. He had left Danville during that time and subsequently returned to live the life of a hermit, seldom venturing outside of his house. By the time he came out of isolation the town had completely changed. One student of Danville history, William Mainwaring, noted that Ficklen's life had a "Rip Van Winkle quality" to it.

---

149 Ibid., p.207-211; *Danville Register*, June 3, 1924.

Born in 1867, Ficklen grew up in Danville. In 1884 he graduated from the University of Virginia and returned home to study for the bar exam. He soon decided that law held no interest for him and moved to New York to become a journalist. There he became an assistant editor for *Munsey's Weekly* and wrote satire for *Life* and *Puck*, three of the nation's most widely read magazines at the time.[150]

Ten years later his parents died. Ficklen returned to Danville to inherit the family money and property. He kept up his writing career by becoming an editor for the *Danville Register* for a year and continuing to work for *Munsey's Weekly*. He also became an editor for the *Danville Free Press* until it went out of business. Soon afterward, *Munsey's Weekly* decided to let his contract expire because he lived in Danville.

Ficklen responded to these setbacks by falling into depression and staying inside his house. Julian Meade wrote:

> Mr. Ficklen, living alone in his dilapidated house, would not sell an inch of his valuable land. For lack of care the place became a jungle of tangled weeds and vines...the house was hidden from the street as though it was lost in a wilderness of green: it was said to be haunted and the ladies who lived nearby could not keep cooks, so frightened were most Negroes by the very thought of this Ficklen's Field where spirits were said to walk after dark and the groans of the dead broke the silence of the night. The only colored people who went near the place were a tribe from Poor House Hill known as the dirt-eaters. These Negroes, mostly fat, dusky-faced women with fallen stomachs and drooping breasts, ate clumps of red clay every morning of their lives and there was no dirt in all Pittsylvania County so good to their particular taste as the red clay that came from under a certain

---

150 Ibid., pp.212-215.

bank on the southeastern side of the haunted field. Their stomachs so craved this delicacy that, to the amazement of all other Negroes from Red Alley to Crooktown, they ventured to fill their baskets with the sweet dirt from the hiding place of ghosts and haunts.

For a long time Mr. Ficklen was a part of this picture. Whenever he ventured forth from the wilderness he carried a small leather satchel, which was said to contain every mystery and device of the devil. Nobody saw him without his satchel and nobody dared to ask him what he bore so faithfully at his side.[151]

According to Meade, "There were two happenings to make the landowner more human in the eyes of the town." First Ficklen moved out of the ramshackle house and into "a house with panes in the windows and no jungle to screen it from the public." Beyond that, "What shocked the town most," Meade wrote, "was that, after a brief courtship Mr. Ficklen married one of the loveliest and gentlest ladies ever to live along the Dan. One explanation was seized upon: the lovely lady was uncommonly learned and she had married a man whose quantity of learning, whatever its quality of usefulness may or may not have been, was beyond dispute."[152]

Ficklen married Mary Tucker, who at twenty-four was half his age, in 1916. His move and marriage cheered his spirits and sparked him to become more involved with the people around him. Ficklen embraced the interests of the people and became critical of Dan River Mills, attitudes that were once popular in 1900.

In 1921 Harry Ficklen secured a license to hold a carnival at "Ficklen's Field," a vacant plot of land near Schoolfield. Ficklen found himself under attack by Dan River and its representatives who didn't want their employees going outside of the mill village for amusement. Schoolfield and H. R. Fitzgerald feared

151 Meade, p. 50.
152 Ibid. pp. 50-51.

that the carnival would encourage drinking and cause rampant immorality.

The Retail Merchants Association, the local Law and Order League, and Schoolfield residents signed a petition asking Mayor Harry Wooding to rescind the license. The mayor said that it was too late to do that, although he now regretted approving it. Even though the carnival went as planned and proved to be a success, Ficklen decided to get back at his critics. He scheduled a "free speech" day to cap off the festival and promised to headline the event with a response to his opponents.[153]

More than one thousand people showed up to hear Ficklen talk. Among them were "some of Danville's best known people" and "a large percentage of Schoolfield people." They came to what, according to the *Danville Register*, was "as frank and direct and outspoken as any public address ever heard here."

Ficklen said that he "had no aspirations of any kind but for a quiet life," but now "they are shelling the woods and the general has come out." After quickly referencing his rights as a property owner, he asked, "Am I my brother's keeper?" Ficklen noted that this biblical phrase has been used to sow "the seeds of a false doctrine which has been foisted upon the people and its meaning quite distorted." He recalled, "Cain had slain Abel and the Almighty, on asking Cain where his brother was, had received an evasive reply, that he did not know." Ficklen said he analyzed the biblical story and added that all he would have to say would be in contradiction to the "pseudo doctrine that man is his brother's keeper."

Ficklen then spoke against "informal chaperonage" and dictates to "what one should do and what one should like." Conceding that carnivals "are a low order of entertainment and they bring groups of undesirable camp followers," he noted that when Dan River Mills held a carnival several months earlier at Schoolfield, nobody complained. "On that occasion there were no efforts,"

---

153 Mainwaring, pp. 216-217.

he said, "to stop it and no signs of remorse on the part of those who allowed it."

He then displayed to the crowd signed petitions that were delivered to the mayor in opposition to his carnival. Dismissing one signed by the "citizens of Schoolfield," he said, "There are no citizens in Schoolfield since it is neither a city or a town." Instead it is a "baronial estate." Noting that the signatures on the petition were filled by "pure and estimable ladies" who did welfare work for the mill, Ficklen mocked a line in the petition that said his carnival would be "especially harmful to the young womanhood and manhood of the community." He asked, "How could these ladies know about corruption of manhood on Ficklen's field unless they were there?" He then said that the other signers of the petition were foremen and managers and proved the document's worthlessness by observing that it had only eighty-three signatures at a time when Schoolfield had a population of 7,500.

Ficklen zeroed in on the name of H. R. Fitzgerald, the president of Dan River Mills. He is a "well-known and admirable man, head of the milling enterprise," but "Jay Gould once stated that he was a Democrat in a Democratic district, a Republican in a Republican district, but an Erie Railroad man all of the time," Ficklen said. Ficklen then directed himself to the people of Schoolfield.

"I am not talking to the higher class, which sneezes when someone else takes snuff," he said. "You are living in a community unique in America," he continued, "in that it has no popular form of government." The mills were built outside of Danville to avoid taxation and in Schoolfield they "own all of the land and there are no property holders who get together and call for a republican form of government," he argued. Ficklen asked the crowd, "Do you want a real government" or do you want to obey "the mandate of a small group of men?" Danville was the last capital of the Confederacy but now should be called the "first Capital of Industrial Autocracy," he stated.

Ficklen closed his remarks by speaking directly to the people of Danville. He pointed out to them that the people of Schoolfield used the city's utilities, but paid little of its taxes. "Your town is being taken by storm," he warned. Ficklen traced the methods of attack "by the dissemination of stock among people of standing for purposes of influencing their bearing toward the mill's future."[154]

Over the next decade Harry Ficklen returned to the same ideas and principles that he expounded in these two speeches over and over again. He believed that Dan River Mills dominated Danville and controlled public opinion. Consequently, free speech and thought disappeared. The Good Government Club operated as a custodial form of government and proxy for the textile company. As a result, a few held power and everyone else was expected to obey. According to Ficklen, the mills had already "helped to reduce the morale of a game little city, of quondam tobacco primacy, to the dead level of a pestiferously paternalist and standardized mill village—where the South buries its Anglo-Saxons—and where men, not owning the soil, their children after them, are likely to become cogs grinding only for private greed that is camouflaged with the badges of benevolence or even the regalia of religion."

Ficklen decided that the only way to break the power of Dan River Mills would be for Danville to annex Schoolfield as that would bring real government to the people living in Schoolfield and make them citizens again. First, though, Danville would have to enforce its election laws. Although Virginia had adopted the secret ballot, Ficklen claimed that there were no enclosed voting booths in Danville. That way people were discouraged from voting and those who did were being supervised, he asserted. If voters weren't protected "from the onslaught of the spying foreman, the half-baked, the lambs, the claquers, the crumb-seekers, the healers and the parasites," he asked, "who can tell but what the Lord will hearken in him so that public opinion will really enact itself?"[155]

Although election officials assured closed-booth voting in the election, Ficklen lost his 1924 run for city council. He captured

---

154 *Danville Register*, April 5, 1921.
155 Mainwaring, pp. 221-222.

only 413 out of 2,000 votes cast. Thanks to the poll tax and re-stricted electorate, few people voted, and those who did often had their poll taxes paid for by people already on the city council or their supporters. However, Ficklen wasn't the only opposition candidate in the 1924 election. A slate of candidates calling itself "The Citizens Ticket" ran on the promise of representing "people from all walks of life." It included two members of the old bicam-eral council and Dr. Henry Wiseman, who had been the sole op-position candidate in 1920.

The *Danville Register* and the *Bee* also joined in opposition against the Good Government Club. Rorer A. James, Jr., the own-er of both papers, initially supported the club, but had become disgusted with some of its tactics. In the previous year the city council initiated a bond referendum to construct new schools. After the voters defeated the measure, the Good Government Club tried to get allies in the General Assembly to change the city's charter so that it wouldn't have to hold any referenda to issue bonds.

When word of the Good Government Club's machinations spread, Rorer A. James, Jr., held a demonstration in opposition. The *Bee* portrayed the meeting as a spontaneous revolt "against a unique form of paternalism and against the policy of forcing on the public what certain gentlemen think is best of less enlightened brethren." The club's city council members backed down.

The incident motivated James to publish a series of articles summarizing the operations of the Good Government Club in his papers. The articles were not much different from Ficklen's speeches about the club, although they didn't name any names or mention Dan River Mills as Ficklen had. The *Danville Register* called the club an "inner circle—a small group of ostensibly well-meaning men who believed that the people of Danville were incapable of governing themselves." The club's "nucleus" was "aug-mented gradually and quietly through the personal efforts of cer-tain original projectors, and embraced me and my wife and my son, John, and his wife, so to speak." Here was "missionary work in high places" and an "endorsement faction." At the same time the *Danville Bee* derided the Good Government club as the elite "Council of Nine."[156]

As Election Day approached, the newspapers stepped up their attacks against the elites. The *Danville Register* reported that the club's leaders had met privately at the Danville Golf Club and had refused to divulge who paid for the dinner. The paper then singled out individual Good Government Club city councilmen for criticism. It pointed out that B. J. Hurd was not even a registered voter and had failed to pay his poll tax. Guy Walter and W. E. Gardner used the council for graft, owning companies that were paid for "hauling" in violation of city ordinances. Another council member's business partner sold the city four old mules for $1,200, although the paper didn't think they were worth $200 all together. "If this is good government, God save the city," the paper lamented.

Due to the press attacks three of the nine incumbent Good Government Club members declined to run for re-election in 1924. Nonetheless, with replacement candidates, the club retained full control of the council. Its lowest vote winner, B. J. Hurd, received 1,081 votes, a hundred more than the best competitor from the Citizen's Ticket. Like Harry Ficklen, the opposition candidates were hampered by the small electorate and lost.[157]

Two years later the opposition scored a victory against the Good Government Club thanks to a stormy issue that brought out the voters. The city council decided to put the city's power companies up for sale and received a bid from the Appalachian Power Company for $2.75 million. Even though the local papers supported the council's action, linking the sale of the power plants to attracting more industries to Danville, the Good Government Club unwittingly unleashed an army of critics, with Harry Ficklen leading the attack.

---

156 Ibid., pp. 225-229.
157 Ibid., pp. 231-232.

Ficklen charged that the Appalachian Power Company would "swallow us alive." Three hundred people joined Ficklen in forming the Citizen's Protective Association. They believed that the city's power utilities were an inheritance from their forefathers that should not be sold. James Wilson, who helped form the organization, dismissed the Chamber of Commerce for trying to promote the sale. "I resent as a citizen having paid hirelings and boosters to come and try to persuade our citizens to vote the birthright away," he said. The CPA members also argued that the utilities were actually worth six million and claimed that the Appalachian would eventually raise power rates if they captured them.

The issue was placed before the voters in a referendum. Almost 30 percent more people voted on the issue than had voted in the last city council election, a testimony to the issue's importance for the people of Danville and the strong feelings it created. In all, 1,412 voted against it and 1,161 voted for it. The referendum drew the most support in the same areas of Danville that were Good Government strongholds. Those against it were most likely to live in North Danville, the same area that opposed eliminating the ward system earlier.

The election didn't bury the issue. Six months later the Good Government Club city council members brought it up for vote again. The voters once again rejected the referendum. This time, though, 500 more people voted in the election. The CPA decided to become a permanent organization and also decided to run its own candidate for the Virginia General Assembly. That way they could amend the city's charter to prevent the sale of the utilities. They chose none other than Harry Ficklen as their candidate.

In 1928 Ficklen won a seat in the House of Delegates. Three days after he arrived, he introduced a series of bills that would bring a revolution to Danville if they passed. One forbade the sale of the city's utilities without the approval of two-thirds of the city's voters. Another called for the election of school board members. More importantly, he also introduced a bill that would bring back ward representation to the city council. This bill aimed to turn back the clock and smash the electoral changes made by the Good Government Club.

As historian William Mainwaring noted, "Ficklen's legislative package caused an uproar back in Danville." The wheels of the Good Government Club spun and the Chamber of Commerce, School Board, city council, Business and Professional Women's Club, PTA, and Rotary and Kiwanis clubs sent people to Richmond to voice their opposition to Ficklen in the General Assembly. A. M. Aiken, the city attorney, said that Ficklen sought to make his home the most "manhandled city in the world." Ficklen in turn called his opponents "poppy cock and moonshine."

The General Assembly's legislative committee voted down Ficklen's utility bill and shelved the rest of his legislation. The *Danville Register* blamed his defeat on his personality and failure to compromise. A few months later, however, he managed to sponsor a compromise bill that required approval by half of the city's voters in order to sell off the utilities, which passed.[158]

Back in Danville, the CPA elected six out of nine candidates to the city council; however, in the next election, the Good Government Club regained control of every council seat. With the power issue fading into the sunset, fewer voters went to the polls. The election was so quiet that the club didn't even make any public stands.

The Good Government Club maintained its grip on Danville until the mid-1940s. Its only opposition between 1920 and World War II came from Harry Ficklen and the CPA and that lasted for only a few years. The club maintained its power through a small electorate, the backing of Dan River Mills and the country club set, and through the power of machine politics. City council members occasionally paid the poll taxes of supporters while those who had jobs for the city found themselves dependent on them. Only the temporary surge in voting caused by the utility issue could dislodge their power for a brief period of time.[159]

---

158 Ibid., pp.240-249; *Danville Register*, January 26, 1928.
159 Mainwaring, p.253.

The Good Government Club outlived Harry Ficklen. After his sojourn in the General Assembly he ran for mayor of Danville in 1928 and 1932. Both times he lost. After his wife died in 1929 he sank into depression. Soon afterward, his creditors forced him to sell his inheritance and he became penniless. In 1935 he died in the Western State Hospital in Staunton Virginia.[160]

Julian Meade lamented his passing:

> When he spoke a decrepit, wrinkled, toothless old man disappeared and you could see the smart, wise-cracking, gentlemanly young blade of the eighties who set out from Danville for the big city just as we who were restless and perverse wanted to do today. All he needed was a starting-point and he would look away wistfully as he recalled the vanished years. He lived almost entirely in the past. Who could blame him? What was the present worth? His lovely wife had died and with her went the best of his life. Taxes and debts and misfortunes had bereft him of his property and now he existed meanly in a furnished room. His health had gone, too, and there was nothing precious left save what he had cherished in a well-remembered past.[161]

160 Ibid., p.261.
161 Meade, p.52.

CHAPTER THREE: Fitzgerald's Dream: *The Rise and Fall of Industrial Democracy*

In 1918 R.A. Schoolfield stepped down as president of Dan River Mills at the age of sixty-five. Harrison Robertson Fitzgerald, the son of mill founder Thomas Fitzgerald, took his place. Although Schoolfield continued to serve as chairman of Dan River's board of directors, Harrison Fitzgerald took over the day-to-day operations of the company. Within years his name became synonymous with the company in ways that Schoolfield's never did.

Fitzgerald began working for the mill company in 1890 as an errand boy. After thirteen years he ascended the management ranks to become the company's treasurer and Schoolfield's personal assistant. Schoolfield personally groomed him to take his place as president. Schoolfield later wrote:

> In past years past, Mr. Fitzgerald has been very efficient and his labors added very materially to the success of the Mills. In his young manhood, on account of his ability, faithfulness, and fidelity I rendered him all the support possible, for which I was criticized, even by his father, there being more or less jealousy among my friends on account of my support of him.[162]

---

162 Robert E King, *Robert Addison Schoolfield: A Biographical History of the Leader of Danville, Virginia's Textile Mills During their first Fifty Years* (Richmond: William Byrd Press, 1979), p.100.

Like Schoolfield, Fitzgerald was a stern and pious man. He taught a Bible class at Mount Vernon Methodist Church and raised five daughters. At the turn of the century he began to go deaf and by the 1920s could barely hear at all. He compensated by reading lips and using a pencil and paper when that failed. When he used the telephone he had an assistant listen in and mouth the words heard on the other line to him.

Before he succeeded Schoolfield, Fitzgerald supervised Dan River's employee "welfare" programs. He began the company's first educational night school and organized the programs that accompanied Schoolfield village. By the time he became president, the company's workforce underwent a subtle transformation.

When Dan River first opened up, factory work was new to its employees, who had left farms to work at the mill. They brought their family work unit to the factory and for necessity didn't hesitate to hire out their children so that all could earn a combined "family wage." Throughout the South most textile workers had been young adults or children. In 1900, 14 percent of Southern mill hands were under the age of fifteen, while 22 percent were between sixteen and twenty-four. However, by 1920 only 4 percent of these workers were under fifteen. A generation grew up in the mill.

That made for a more experienced, productive, and stable workforce. It also meant a more male-dominated workforce. In its earliest years, male workers often left Southern textile manufacturing to return to farming. By the 1920s, young men who were twenty-five or older and were still working in textiles were unlikely to ever leave. "It was not that they were trapped by debts or kept in ignorance of the outside world," wrote historian Gavin Wright, "but if they had no agricultural experience whatever by their mid-twenties it was difficult to start anew at that age."[163]

Greater worker productivity generated more profits for Dan River Mills. In turn the company paid out higher wages than it

---

163 Gavin Wright, *Old South, New South: Revolutions in the Southern Economy Since the Civil War* (Baton Rouge: Louisiana State University Press, 1986), pp. 140-141.

did before 1900 and offered its employees "welfare" programs. Despite better conditions, many people outside of the textile industry claimed that the mill village turned men into pitiful serfs.

In 1941 Southern author W. J. Cash, for example, wrote:

> And to this is must be added that working conditions in the Southern Cotton mills were extremely unfavorable. Men and women and children were cooped up for most of their waking lives in the gray light of glazed windows, and in rooms which were never effectively ventilated, since cotton yarns will break in the slightest draft—in rooms which, because of the use of artificial humidification, were hardly less than perpetual steam baths.
>
> The harvest was soon at hand. By 1900 the cotton-mill worker was a pretty distinct type in the South; a type in some respects perhaps inferior to even that of the old poor white; which in general had this to begin with. A dead-white skin, a sunken chest, and stooping shoulders were earmarks of the breed. Chinless faces, microcephalic foreheads, rabbit teeth, goggling dead-fish eyes, rickety limbs, and stunted bodies abounded—over and beyond the limit of their prevalence in the countryside. The women were characteristically stringy-haired and limp of breast at twenty, and shrunken hags at thirty or forty. And the incidence of tuberculosis, of insanity and epilepsy, and above all, of pellagra, the curious vitamin-deficiency disease, which is peculiar to the South, was increasing.[164]

Although Cash's statement is a bit overblown, it was common for people to claim that textile mills trapped people in poverty or to compare them with baronial estates. In response to such criticisms by the Southern Industrial Conference, a group of clergymen who sought to reform textile mills, Fitzgerald wrote a long

---

164 W.J. Cash, *The Mind of the South* (New York: Vintage Books, 1991), p.200.

letter in which he defended the mill village system and idealized it. It is noteworthy, because it shows how he personally viewed the system and his own role in it. He wrote:

> Our first mill was built in 1882, at which time my father and the three Schoolfield brothers, together with two or three other friends, started a development for the express purpose of affording work to the poor families of the community, who were having a hard time.
>
> Of course the mill immediately became a center to which all of these unfortunate people would flock, and instead of the mill being responsible for the conditions among them, it proved to be a godsend in offering them an opportunity for employment, which was the first and most important step and what they needed more than anything else to obtain food and clothes and a reasonable measure of independence.
>
> We built additional mills at intervals of a few years apart until the Riverside group of seven mills was completed...instead of a large surplus of help we had about digested the supply in our immediate community, so that it became necessary to develop the village of Schoolfield. We had to draw upon the mountain districts of the Piedmont section. I would not now attempt to describe the conditions that existed among virtually all of these families in their state of run-down poverty and ignorance, and eking out a precarious existence on mountain farms. Some of the worst cases of disease and a long chain of evils and vices that had grown into their methods of living, were enough to shock the sensibilities of anyone who loves humanity.
>
> While it had been our custom to promote educational work among our operatives in the city and to assist in their churches and social affiliations, we soon recognized that it was a question of business necessity to begin

at the very bottom with day nurseries, kindergardens, primary departments, as well as district nursing and medical department, if we were to ever develop a nucleus of capable and efficient workers. For anyone to have seen their methods of living, cooking, and sanitary surroundings they would have wondered how anyone could live under those circumstances, and it is true that the death rate was high and the health rate extremely low.

Furthermore, they were proud as well as ignorant, and any attempt to get at them in other than a very practical way would have been an utter failure. It required several years in which to make any real progress in this direction, but having laid the foundation we kept persistently at it and did not hesitate to gradually broaden and enlarge the scope of our work as fast as circumstances justified.

After a few years we could begin to see some of the results of this work and I may say that after ten or fifteen years we had virtually succeeded in transforming the entire community and, incidentally, in developing a core of operatives of intelligence and efficiency, which, in our opinion, has more than repaid all that it cost, to say nothing of the infinite satisfaction of having some small share in the transformation of so many lives and in bringing happiness and reasonable prosperity to thousands of people who otherwise would never have had it.

As to the criticism of the mill village and the suggestion that it represents some system of serfdom, etc., the idea is so ridiculous as to show on its face that the author of the suggestion knows nothing about it. I do not suppose there is a more independent or self-asserting class of people anywhere who know better what they want or who represent a more genuine type of Democracy than will be found among the mill villages of the South.[165]

---

165 Robert Sidney Smith, *Mill on the Dan* (North Carolina: Duke University Press, 1960), pp.242-243.

Fitzgerald believed that during the industrial revolution "one of the great evils" was the tendency of manufacturers to treat workers "exactly as they would machinery" and "obtain it at the lowest possible price and get just as much out of it as they could." He idealized the mill village as a better alternative and at times saw it as the most important accomplishment in his life.[166]

Industrial Democracy

The mill village never became the oasis of harmony Fitzgerald imagined it to be. There never was a time in which everyone was content in the mills, because the mill village system still had the profit motive at the center of it, which depended on extracting as much labor as possible from its workers. In 1917 Hattie Hylton, who directed the "welfare" department at Dan River Mills, told Fitzgerald of spreading unrest. Many employees, she wrote, felt:

> That they were not fairly treated by their "boss." That the bosses try to drive them and they say they can be led a long way, but will not be driven. They also say that this driving method is not true of any other mill. Many say that they are sorry to leave and do so on that account alone, as they cannot stand it.
>
> Another reason often given, is that they can make so much more elsewhere, particularly at Spray, Leaksville, and Draper, and that they can live much cheaper at either of these places.
>
> There has been growing dissatisfaction, very freely expressed, that there is no chance for a man "to get anywhere" in the mill. That there is no system of promotion. That when a man is wanted to take any position of trust that he is always brought in from some other mill.

Hylton blamed most of these problems on middle management:

---

166 Ibid., p.263.

> Your second hands are variously charged with impu-
> rity and profanity, with driving, over-bearing, and unsympa-
> thetic administration of their powers, with discrimination
> unfairly against their best help because of jealousy... the
> superintendents and overseers are censured for backing
> up the second hands, without due investigation of the
> merits of every case, so that often acts of injustice are
> committed and allowed to pass.
>
> While your own, and Mr. Schoolfield's attitude toward
> the Welfare Work for your employees is understood by
> the people to be a lofty and noble one...the indifference
> of the superintendents and overseers of every degree is
> not understood.[167]

Each employee who believed he received unfair treatment
became a potential union member. Just after Fitzgerald became
president of Dan River Mills, he informed Schoolfield that two or
three attempts by "outside parties" to organize the mills had been
made. "I am glad to say that we have apparently frustrated each
attempt," he wrote. However, a small group of skilled employees
organized themselves into the Loom Fixer's Southern Association
of the American Federation of Labor.[168]

Although these employees stayed quiet, their very existence
must have troubled the company's management. Caught between
employees who wanted better conditions and a need to get as
much profit out of them as possible, Fitzgerald found an answer
to these contradictions of business in a book called *Man to Man*.

Written by John Leitch, the book proposed an alternative to
unions or autocratic managerial rule. Calling his plan Industrial
Democracy, Leitch argued that companies should model themselves after the federal government and create a House of
Representatives, Senate, and cabinet. The workers would elect
the House of Representatives. The Senate would be made up of

---

167 Ibid., pp. 261-262.
168 Ibid., p. 263.

overseers, while the cabinet would consist of the company's executives. Leitch claimed that employees could find a voice inside of the Industrial Democracy system and would thereby feel no need to organize themselves with unions.

Fitzgerald bought a hundred copies of the book and sent them to key employees and friends. Like Leitch, he saw the plan as an alternative to unions. Speaking to the Blue Ridge Industrial Conference, President Fitzgerald argued that unions "have certainly brought a great many blessings that labor would not otherwise have gotten. Shorter hours, more pay, and better working conditions are undoubted products of militant unionism, and it not only had the approval of fair minded men and women everywhere, but for a long time the battles that they waged almost invariably commanded the sympathy and applause of the disinterested public."

However, unions were now "simply carrying out the same principle, in virtually the same way…that the employer did when he tried to get out of labor all that he could and give us little in return," he continued. For Fitzgerald, Leitch's Industrial Democracy harmonized the interests of labor and management:

> Industrial Democracy is not, as some have supposed, a paternalistic or socialist theory; it does not mean democratization in the sense of government ownership of railroads, etc. It is merely the application of true democratic principles to industry. Ethically it means a square deal in wages and working conditions; in reality it is a system of self government in which the operatives have a voice in all matters pertaining to their welfare.[169]

Fitzgerald single handedly introduced Industrial Democracy to Dan River Mills. On July 30, 1919, he announced to the board of directors that it "is a system of self government fashioned

---

169 Ibid., pp.264-265.

on the order Federal Constitution and National Government." He argued for its necessity, noting that "the whole atmosphere, especially for the past few months" has been "surcharged with labor troubles. Unions have been organized all over the South, and with the backing of the Government Labor Departments, all of whom seem to champion any demands that the Unions make, it has been extremely difficult to keep our situation here free from complications."[170]

Unions posed a mortal threat to the mill village system, which depended on the absolute authority of management and President Fitzgerald. In the company-owned mill village, any issue that became disputed by organized workers could potentially call into question the entire system of corporate control, because Fitzgerald and Dan River not only set the wages of its workers like any other company, but also sought to regulate their lives inside the village. If Dan River were to bargain with workers organized through a union of their own it would mean the loss of the mill village and Fitzgerald's view of himself as its benevolent ruler.

The Industrial Democracy plan helped Fitzgerald's continue his adulation of the mill village. In fact it promised to give the workers a voice in the company's affairs, or at least the appearance of one, while protecting his authority. However, some doubted it from the beginning. Although he went along with it, Schoolfield privately told Fitzgerald that its "principles" made little sense and any plan based on them would become unworkable.[171]

In theory the House of Representatives, which consisted of 117 elected workers, gave employees a mechanism to create changes in the workplace. In practice, this was very limited due to the fact that Fitzgerald could veto all legislation they issued without any appeal. Nevertheless, the mill hands debated bills ranging from such measures as installing drinking fountains and better lighting to petty demands such as a failed bid to force "the Greeks" to lose their lease for their popular Schoolfield lunch

---

170 Ibid., pp. 265-266.
171 King, p.99.

restaurant. The workers did pass a segregation ordinance that denied blacks employment "in any department or capacity other than sweepers, scourers, or floor cleaners, or janitors.[172]

At first the mill workers welcomed Industrial Democracy. Clifton Parrot, who served as the "Speaker of the House of Representatives" said the chief reasons for its acceptance was that "the employees in the past never had one word to say about their surroundings, and the conditions under which they should work." Industrial Democracy, however limited it may have been, gave the workers hope that things could be made better.[173]

Inevitably, some workers tried to stretch Industrial Democracy beyond its limits to discover that President Fitzgerald held the ultimate authority. An anonymous petition circulated on the factory floor demanding that the House of Representatives pass a bill to issue the company's stock to its employees. Fitzgerald quickly denounced the petition as "a breach of etiquette and a direct violation of the rules of Industrial Democracy." He called the act "misleading and absurd" since only the stockholders and directors had the right to deal with questions of stock ownership.[174]

As part of the Industrial Democracy program Fitzgerald authorized the publication of a newspaper called *Progress*. Published by the Welfare Department, *Progress* extolled the virtues of Dan River Mills and Industrial Democracy. Its first issue led off with the following: "Howdy! Well, here's a little surprise for you, another result of Industrial Democracy—your own paper…Things will be written so you can understand them…Let's proceed to issue the liveliest, most interesting paper in the country." It included the following poem:

---

172 Smith, pp.269-272.
173 Robert E King, *A Cultural Innovation that Failed: The Rise and Fall of "Industrial Democracy" at the Riverside and Dan River Cottons Mills, Danville, Virginia, 1919-1930* (Ph.D. Thesis: University of Pennsylvania, 1978), pp.36-37.
174 Smith, pp.275-276.

No more we'll toil by rule of might
    At Schoolfield and Riverside
We each shall live the rule of right
    At Schoolfield and Riverside
True glory lies in noble life.
Not sullen scorn nor envious strife.
Nor where oppression's law is rife.
    At Schoolfield and Riverside.
Justice shall always lead the way
    At Schoolfield and Riverside.
Democracy shall have the sway
    At Schoolfield and Riverside
No man shall claim another's toil,
Nor wrong his brother on thy soil.
Each man shall haughty spirits foil
    At Schoolfield and Riverside
Thy sheets and ginghams lead the world,
    At Schoolfield and Riverside
Nor shall our banners e'er be furled
    At Schoolfield and Riverside
Some day each brother's toil shall cease,
From work in rest shall find release,
Till then we'll have Industrial Peace
    At Schoolfield and Riverside[175]

Fitzgerald also added one key component to Industrial Democracy: an economy dividend. Borrowing this idea from the Leitch book, the economy dividend consisted of a sum of money added on top of the hourly wage that varied with the efficiency of the average worker. Based on the cost per pound of cloth, the dividend attempted to encourage worker efficiency and cooperation. As President Fitzgerald explained it:

---

175 Ibid., p. 273.

This is how it works. Suppose I were the employer and
you the employee. We get together in a friendly way and
agree to act on the square with each other. I am to pay
you the market wage—which is easy to determine—and
I am also to give you the opportunity to increase that by
individual effort. At the same time I am to share 50-50
in the results of improved production. This plan is just a
mutual interchange of good.

During times of idleness the dividend shrank. Although it always grew smaller during holidays, especially Christmas when the
factory usually shut down for a week, Fitzgerald argued that dividends were held down by "those who allow bad work to get un-
corrected, those who are unwilling to stretch where necessary to
make their work more effective, or who fail to use their brain in
an honest and earnest effort to help reduce the cost or improve
the quality and enhance the quantity of production."[176]

The Crisis of Industrial Democracy

Despite Fitzgerald's visions of altruism, the "welfare" system fell
apart on the shores of reality. No matter how many programs
Dan River Mills created for its employees, the company was still a
business that depended on profits to maintain itself and please its
stockholders. In turn for their loyalty the workers also expected
to be treated decently and receive their own fare share. When the
Southern textile industry slumped during the 1920s both sides
turned against the system and Fitzgerald fell into despondency.

Textiles boomed in the South during World War I. Between
1900 and 1926 the number of spindles in Southern Cotton Mills
increased from five million to eighteen million. However, by late
1920 the World War I economic upswing ran its course and de-
mand for textile products declined throughout the United States.
Prices for cotton products also dropped, placing deflationary
pressures on textile plants. Many mills went bankrupt and those

---

176 Ibid., p. 285-286.

that weathered the storm were forced to lower prices and cut costs in order to maintain profit margins. Labor held the biggest cost for textile plants and cutting costs meant raising worker productivity and lowering their pay.

On September 20, 1920, Fitzgerald told Dan River's board of directors that "for the past two weeks we have been in the midst of a very drastic revision in the cotton goods markets, prices for practically all lines of cottons having gone down to an extent varying from 20 percent to 33 1/3 percent." He then informed the mill's workers, through the House of Representatives, that a 22.72 percent reduction in wages was necessary or the mills would have to shut down. [177]

Fitzgerald's message set off a storm of debate in the House of Representatives. One speaker asked for a four-day week with wage rates unchanged. Another one believed that the company's surplus "rightfully, but not legally belongs to the operatives who earned it." Finally, one man who supported the wage cuts won the day. He said he had "studied the situation over and prayed about it" and believed the legislature should leave the matter of wages to the president and "thank him for the privilege of working." It had no other choice.

Eleven days after the employees agreed to lower their pay, Fitzgerald asked for and got a $20,000 pay raise from the board of directors. Over the next nine years Fitzgerald cut wages three more times. After each cut posters went up throughout the mills informing workers of their representatives' decisions. In 1921 after one wage cut he said, "Instead of complaining as if we had experienced a hardship, when in fact we have had steady employment and have received more money from the same period than any other similar industry in the United States, we should thank God for the blessing we have." Three years later he lowered wages again and said that the decision had been approved by the workers, because a "cooperative spirit resided in them." [178]

---

177 King, *Schoolfield*, pp. 101-103.
178 Smith, pp. 279-280; Burton White, Jr., <u>Cotton Mills and Organized Labor, Danville Virginia 1930-1931</u> (M.A. Thesis: University of North Carolina at Chapel Hill, 1971). p.17.

In 1925 the company hired the Textile Development Corporation to study ways to increase worker productivity. They concluded that using a more uniform filament could cut loom stoppage. This meant that the "weaver could be stretched from forty-eight to sixty-four Draper looms." This would cut the number of weavers in half. Fitzgerald carried out several other efficiency studies over the next five years, with each one resulting in larger workloads for the employees.

It had become clear to workers that Industrial Democracy functioned merely in name. In 1919, its first year, mill hands presented 304 bills to the House of Representatives. Between 1924 and 1925, however, only fifteen bills came up. By 1923 only half of the elected members of the House of Representatives were regularly attending meetings. Meetings became only perfunctory—a reading of minutes, a roll call, and then a trip to a movie. The Economy Dividend became the only functional component of Industrial Democracy, a situation Fitzgerald confessed to the Danville Rotary Club: "I am frank to say that in the absence of this practical feature and with human nature in its present stage of development, the system would not get very far."[179]

Although Industrial Democracy seemed to be fading in Danville, Fitzgerald gave outside observers the impression that it was thriving and encouraged other textile companies to copy it. The industry journal *Textile World* called it "as vital a factor in the employer-employee relations in Danville today as it has ever been." In 1929 Fitzgerald sent Clifton Parrott to the annual meeting of the National Association of Cotton Manufacturers where he delivered a speech written by Fitzgerald extolling the virtues of Industrial Democracy.[180]

By 1924, though, it was undeniable to people inside Dan River that times were changing no matter how much Fitzgerald tried to pretend otherwise. The first annual loss in the company's history occurred in 1924. Robert Schoolfield, who represented

179 Smith, pp.268, 290; White, p.21-22.
180 Smith, p.291.

stockholders as Dan River's chairman of the board, used the occasion to write Fitzgerald a letter telling him that "the time has come when we should stop, look, and listen." In a follow-up letter he warned, "We have been too extravagant. Prosperity has turned our heads and gotten away from us. I will assume all responsibility up to this time, but from now on I am not willing to do so. I feel that there must be a radical change, in fact that it is imperative if we are to conduct our business in a successful way."

Schoolfield claimed that "the overheard expense is too great, salaries too high, the Welfare Department is costing too much money, your old and faithful operatives have been out of work or on short time, and their labor is the productive feature and has to take care of large expenses that are non-productive...We are not going to be on a good foundation until these things are taken into consideration and put on a more equitable basis." In response, Fitzgerald argued that the best way to control expenses was to focus solely on worker wages.

Fitzgerald told Schoolfield, "I'm confident that we need have no fear, if we simply work together and do our best to help." The two were facing a difference of opinion. Schoolfield wanted management to cut their pay along with the workers and wanted to lower the overhead expenses in the Welfare Department as much as possible instead of lowering the wages of operatives. Schoolfield challenged Fitzgerald to cut management wages by 10 percent and, when he took no action, Schoolfield voluntarily lowered his own pay by 15 percent.

In future correspondence Fitzgerald held his line and continually argued for Schoolfield to go along with his more "modern ideas," while Schoolfield expressed doubts over the validity of Industrial Democracy. At one point he argued that the economy dividend should be eliminated in return for higher wages, an act that he thought employees would favor, but would have eliminated the only remaining functional part of Industrial Democracy. It seems likely that Fitzgerald did not want to face the fact that Industrial Democracy was not working. He had single-handedly brought it to Dan River and campaigned for other textile companies to copy it. It had become a part of his self-image as a benevolent employer.[181]

In 1926 Schoolfield became so frustrated that he sent a long letter to all of the directors of Dan River. It said:

> The Mill management has put great stress on the faithfulness of our organization. This, I think in instances has been remarkable. They [workers] have quietly voted reductions in their wages when a like or greater reduction should have been made higher up. In fact I think through the salaries of all the higher-priced ones. But no, that would be out of order [according to Fitzgerald]… It grieves me to the quick when I think about the breakers ahead and see whether we are drifting and how soon we may get there by patting ourself on the shoulders and making plausible talks and speeches comparing ourselves to others, look only at things in a superficial way, see the bright ones, and shut our eyes to the red lights ahead of us.

Fitzgerald took offense to Schoolfield's letter and complained that he "was unwilling to accord to me the support that I or anyone else would be compelled to have in order to succeed." The next year he convinced the other directors to pass a bylaw stripping Schoolfield of any power in the company and giving himself "control over all its affairs." Schoolfield retired in 1930. He talked of retiring earlier, but stayed on the board in fear that if he retired and sold his shares in the company that its stock would collapse.[182]

He warned other board members that Fitzgerald had become a delusional "self-appointed apostle" of Industrial Democracy and believed that he had created so many grievances with the workers that they had become a "bomb that might explode at anytime."

181 King, *Schoolfield*, p. 106-114.
182 Ibid., pp. 117-120.

Schoolfield thought that all they "wanted was sympathetic treatment and not coercion," but were going to turn to union organizers as a recourse.[183]

As the pressures mounted Fitzgerald relied more and more on a small circle of advisers and used his growing hearing loss as an excuse to isolate himself from others. As his workers abandoned Industrial Democracy he grieved that he felt as if he were "drinking hemlock" and began to consult with an astrologer. To some he appeared to be on the verge of a mental breakdown.[184]

Local 199 and the United Textile Workers of America

Schoolfield knew what people outside of Dan River did not know, or in some cases refused to acknowledge. Hidden by the veneer of Industrial Democracy and positive press stories, workers had been agitating for years for better working conditions. Violent labor disputes in the Southern textile industry had erupted throughout the South in such places as Gastonia, Marion, and Elizabethton, but not in Danville. Danville's middle-class citizens often stated that their city was immune to such disputes, because of Dan River's widely admired management, giant size, reputation for higher wages, welfare programs, and Industrial Democracy. Indeed, according to Julian Meade, the company had such high esteem that it wasn't unusual to hear its plants referred to as "the greatest cotton mills in the world" or hear a preacher thank God for them during Sunday church services.[185]

In 1919 a small group of skilled loom fixers organized a chapter of the National Loomfixers' Association of America in Dan River's plants, Local 199. When Industrial Democracy's Senate, made up of the company's overseers, vetoed a bill to provide extra pay for the loom fixers, a group of workers from the association went

---

183 Ibid., pp.45, 56; Robert Addison Schoolfield Papers, 1855-1973, Accession #10325,
     University of Virginia Library, Charlottesville, Virginia.
184 Ibid; New York Times, June 15, 1930.
185 Mainwaring, pp.275-276; Meade, pp.6, 36-37.

directly to Fitzgerald to present their case. He rebuffed them and, in 1925, they again approached him, this time asking for time and a half for overtime. He took this as an "unwelcome surprise" and replied with a three-page letter extolling the advantages of Industrial Democracy and said it would be impossible for the company to operate "according to rules made somewhere else."[186]

It is noteworthy that Fitzgerald spoke with union members in the mills at all. In 1925, J. C. Blackwell, the secretary of the Loom Fixers' Local, sent him a Christmas card thanking him for the "kindly consideration given our claims during the past year, and the numerous courtesies shown our representatives." Blackwell hoped "to cooperate with you to the end that Justice shall prevail between man and man."

By 1928, though, any idea of friendly cooperation disappeared. The combination of repeated wage cuts, a quick increase in efficiency studies, and their application through the "stretch-out" caused the loom fixers to take a bold step. After another disappointing meeting with Fitzgerald, they printed an open letter in the *Danville Bee* to him complaining that money saved from the "stretch-out" had not been fairly distributed between the company and its employees. The extra work threatened to "sap the strength of our men to such an extent that they will be made easy prey to such diseases as Pneumonia, Influenza, and Tuberculosis," they continued. The loom fixers said that they did not want "to make trouble" and recalled that in the past the union committee had "always met with a kind reception from you, though some have lost their jobs soon after the interview for obscure reasons."

Industrial Democracy finally fell completely apart on January 9, 1930. On that day Fitzgerald shocked those who showed up at a regular meeting of the House of Representatives by announcing an immediate 10 percent wage reduction, which also included a 10 percent cut for salaried management. The Speaker of the

---

186 White, p. 18; Smith, pp. 281-282.

House appointed five workers to meet with Fitzgerald to voice their objections. As the meeting concluded the workers told him that they wanted to discuss the wage reduction and take a vote on it. Instead of waiting on them Fitzgerald posted a circular throughout the mill announcing the job cuts, thereby making future meetings of the House of Representatives pointless. L. G. Nunn, a weaver in the mill, wrote a letter to the *Greensboro Daily News* revealing that the majority who opposed the wage cut in the House had been fired, in what many believed was retaliation. He claimed that workers preferred better pay over the welfare facilities Fitzgerald provided.

The Loom Fixers' Local decided to get help in order to organize the entire plant. A group of them went to a convention of the American Federation of Labor and met with William Green to ask for "an experienced organizer." The surprised Green passed their request on to Francis Gorman, the vice president of the United Textile Workers of America (UTWA), who decided to come to Danville and see for himself what was going on.

Once he arrived in Danville, Gorman decided to make Dan River the focus of a drive to unionize Southern textile workers. Just like Samuel Gompers before him, Gorman likely believed that if he were successful other plants in the region would follow. As the industry magazine *American Wool and Cotton Reporter* noted, Dan River "was the most likely place for the United Textile Workers to make their demonstration. It is the biggest mill in the South" and has "found it impossible to keep their operatives steadily employed and impossible to maintain a net income that would justify the maintenance of common stock dividends. Hence, here was the easiest place in the South to find a large number of operatives unemployed or only partially employed and most amenable to the orations and expositions of labor union organizers. And stockholders without dividends are more apt to be critical of mill management." [187]

---

187 Smith, p.292-294; White, p.26.

The Loom Fixers' Local dissolved itself and merged into Local No. 1685 of the UTWA, which now represented all classes of Dan River employees. B. L. Nash became its president and James Blackwell served as its secretary. The two sent a letter to Fitzgerald, which read:

> The workers in the mill want their own union and we ask you why they should not have it. They also want an opportunity to demonstrate to the company that this union will be helpful and not harmful. We believe in collective bargaining and will continue along these lines, but we cannot subscribe to a policy of so-called Industrial Democracy which forces workers downward.[188]

The union attempted to meet with Fitzgerald several times, but each time he rebuffed them. On February 9, 1930, the union held a rally at the Majestic Theater. One thousand workers showed up to hear Francis Gorman, O. E. Woodberry, the publicity director of the AFL, and Mathilda Lindsay, a leading organizer from the South, declare that they were "here to stay." Seven hundred and fifty workers signed up for the union and paid initial dues of one dollar.

In response Fitzgerald put up another poster throughout the mills calling the union an organization led by "foreign agitators." He wrote, "Our system of employee representation contains every element of collective bargaining that has any real merit. We do not desire the employees of the company to be misled by these outsiders for the simple reason that they cause discord and their method of operation depends on agitation and strife. What can such a movement do for you," he asked, "that you do not already have except to take your money in dues to pay a lot of foreign agitators and some few disgruntled, under appreciative, persons who are continually sowing seeds of discord and unhappiness?"[189]

---

188 Tippett, p.214.
189 Smith, pp.299-300.

Robert Meacham, The editor of the *Danville Register* agreed. In an editorial he declared that in Danville "there will be no surrender to the destructive teachings of Communism." Dan River "always placed consideration for its workers first" and Fitzgerald was trying to solve the problems of overproduction "to the best interest of all," he argued. Meacham claimed that the mill workers knew this and would logically "extend their loyal cooperation."[190]

J. C. Blackwell responded with a plea to Fitzgerald. In a personal letter he explained that the union organizers "are not foreign agitators but American citizens delegated by President Green of the American Federation of Labor to assist us. When you say their whole method of operation depends upon agitation and strife we would call to your attention that the officials of the Labor movement have advised workers in the mills to keep calm, that the AFL is not here for strife or strike, but to organize the workers and do business in an orderly manner with justice to employer and employees."

Fitzgerald didn't reply to the letter. Instead he fired Blackwell and fifty-five other workers he saw as "snakes in the grass going out of their way to induce others to join the movement." He hoped that with the "few of the rotten ones" gone things would return back to normal. Fitzgerald also encouraged "loyal" employees to try to dissuade other workers from joining the union and kept up charges that "foreign agitators" led the union. The latter tactic succeeded in making the local Ku Klux Klan suspicious of the Catholic Francis Gorman. The Klan had allowed the union to house its headquarters in Dansylvania Hall, the Klan's meeting place, but now demanded that it be moved.[191]

Fitzgerald's campaign against the union failed to prevent workers from joining it. By March, 1930, 92 percent of them had signed union cards. Fitzgerald held a closed meeting with the other directors of Dan River and gave them a rundown of events. He informed them that the Loom Fixers' Association invited the "labor

---

190 *Danville Register*, January 23, 1930.
191 Mainwaring, p. 282; Smith, p. 305.

organizers and agitators" to "come just at the psychological moment to use our wage reduction as an excuse for organizing a union." The meeting ended with the approval of a statement that the company had "no intention of having any conference or anything whatever to with these organizers."

A few days later Geoffrey Brown, acting as a personal representative of the AFL, came to Fitzgerald's office. He told them that he wanted to discuss "alleged discrimination against your employees because they are members of the union." The mill president quickly told him, "If you come here to discuss matters pertaining to the running of our business, you will have to excuse me. You are neither an employee nor a stockholder of the company and we have nothing whatever to discuss with you." Lines were drawn.[192]

The Undesirables

For the most part, Danville's middle-class citizens remained unaware of the magnitude of the events that were taking place inside the mills and Schoolfield. The local papers mentioned the union and Fitzgerald's position, but none of them gave a clue to the size of the organizing drive or the seriousness of the situation. That changed overnight. As Julian Meade recalled:

> The union had been gathering its forces slowly, but it was not until April before this September that we knew how much was happening within our gates. One perfect afternoon of warm sun and burnished skies the United Textile Workers had staged on Main Street what was probably the greatest labor parade in the history of the South. The line was two miles long. Nearly five thousand workers and their sympathizers marched three abreast. They were led by little Francis Gorman, whose lighthearted mood seemed to be shared by only a part of

---

192 Smith, pp. 308-309.

those who followed in his train: some were sullen, some were bored, some were openly contemptuous of the assembled citizenry who gaped in amazement from sidewalks and porches along the way. Many paraders were dressed in their Sunday best—"best" that was not so fine as local observers reported it to be, for the occasional fur pieces, worn fashionably in the warm weather, were cheap imitations and the silk stockings we heard so much about were not without darns. Some of the girls wore high heels and parading was as difficult for them as it was for cripples with their crutches and mothers who carried babies. Past the Elks Club, past the more prominent Methodist and Baptist churches, past the best homes, the line moved on to the spirited music of a lively band.

The banners of the UTW waved beside the Stars and Stripes. Huge placards flashed by:

WE ARE THE UNDESIRABLES

55 HOURS of WORK FOR $13.50 COULD YOU LIVE ON THAT

DISCHARGED BECAUSE WE JOINED THE UNION

WE WANT AN OPPORTUNITY TO DEMONSTRATE TO OUR EMPLOYERS THAT WE BEAR THEM NO ILL WILL

It had been feared by gloomier spectators that there would be a special demonstration in front of Mr. Fitzgerald's residence. But the workers did no more than stare at the white house where curtains were drawn as though the family had safeguarded themselves from this tumultuous scene.

Near me on the sidewalk two middle-aged women with flat voices had gossiped cheerfully.

"Poor Mr. Fitzgerald, I know he never thought he'd live to see this day. These common people ought to be ashamed of themselves. Just look how many of those mill girls have got on silk hose! Somebody was tellin' me the other day that they won't buy anything but the best grade hose and a friend of mine who knows a clerk in the Schoolfield store says they buy strawberries in March. And here they are grumblin' about $13.50 a week. I don't pay my cook but $3. How much do you pay yours? You do? Well, honey, if the poor whites keep on like this, the next thing we know the niggers will be paradin' around."

"Saints preserve us! But I declare it's awful for these foreign agitators to come stirrin' up trouble in Danville. The police ought to get busy right now."

"You're exactly right. I just can't help thinkin' of Mr. Fitzgerald. He's always been so good to everybody and now it looks like the whole town is fussin' at him. It's not just these laborin' people either. The stockholders are furious because they didn't get any dividends. They say he ought to have cut salaries long before now."

"Well, he certainly has done some whackin' now. He cuts everybody from himself right on down."

"Yes, he used to get $75,000 and now just gets $60,000. Goodness, I can't conceive of that much money!"

"It is a lot of money. But then he's a mighty generous man. Of course, I reckon he's been too extravagant too. You know what they say about his daughter's trousseau, all the finery she bought in New York. They say she spent thousands on that weddin'. Just like money grew on trees."

At this point I had left to follow the paraders to Ballou Park where there was to be speech-making by the visitors. I knew what the rest of the dialogue would have been. Every time that trousseau was described by the disgruntled stockholders or the general public its costly magnificence became more and more incredible. Thousands of dollars they said. The best silk lingerie from Fifth Avenue. Silk chemises and step-ins like movie stars wore. Handkerchiefs that cost ten dollars apiece. And, meanwhile, no dividends for the poor widows whose husbands had seen fit to put their earnings in our local common or preferred. It was true that salaries and wages had been slashed at last and some of the men who made fifteen or twenty thousand would have to be content with less, just as the weavers and doffers, and carders must suffer their ten per cent too. Why single out the fact that a salary of $60,000 was nothing to kick about? Couldn't Fitzgerald get that much from another mill any time he pleaded and, besides, didn't he give away a large part of his earnings to private and public charities?

Thus, as I hurried toward the park, I reviewed in my mind what had been hear-say along the streets. I wondered fearfully what the outcome of all this trouble would be. Ours was the largest independent mill in the South and if the union entered these mill gates you might as well say that their biggest battle was won and that other victories would ensue. Danville, so *The Nation* said, was labor's outpost in the South. The Industrial Democracy which Mr. Fitzgerald founded and nursed had been eulogized far and wide as a happy scheme of cooperation between those who hired and those who labored. It seemed, now, however, that our little world was less secure. Sadly I recalled local-history classes and the time we were kept in after school if we did not know that Danville, with its motto of "Danville Does Things," was the birthplace of Nancy Astor, the largest of loose leaf tobacco markets, and, most particularly, the home of one of the greatest cotton mills in the world.[193]

---

193 Meade, pp.8-12.

The march garnered national attention and columnists across the country viewed the outcome of the union drive in Danville as a cornerstone for the future of unionism in the South. The *New York Daily News Record*, for instance, reported:

> The eyes of the South are on the labor situation in Danville, Virginia, and it seems conceded among mill executives that if the union leaders fail in their present efforts at the Riverside and Dan River Cotton Mills, they have failed in their present campaign.[194]

The *New York Times* sent reporter Anne O'Hare McCormick to cover the story. She interviewed Fitzgerald and found a man in deep despair. "That they should have turned from him and the company union to 'foreign agitators' and strange gods, inviting representatives of the United Textile Union to organize them, is a personal tragedy: Mr. Fitzgerald speaks of 'drinking the hemlock,'" she wrote. Fitzgerald was particularly hurt when the employees in the House of Representatives said that they wanted to abandon the company's welfare system for higher wages. "Perhaps no suggestion could be more shocking," she continued, "to a man who believes he has devoted his life to the betterment of his people."[195]

Julian Meade, while working as a high school teacher of English and French, began to moonlight as a reporter for the United Press covering the labor dispute. He was friends with Fitzgerald's daughter, Harriett, while his father was a regular golf partner of his. He later wrote:

> After I got permission to report the labor dispute, Harriett and I went for a long walk through the autumn-colored woods along Stony Creek and it was then that we aired our views. I had no fear of talking frankly. Although

---

194 White, p.68.
195 *New York Times*, June 15, 1930.

Harriet's natural devotion to her father might have kept her from looking at this quarrel with the same discernment and tolerance she had in most matters, she was too intelligent to close her mind entirely to the workers' story. She was considerably more open-minded to the union's argument than were the majority of Danville citizens, many of whom could see no further than the issue of dividends and stocks. We debated amicably as we walked along the moss-covered edges of the creek.

"We've got to look at this thing straight," I said. "There are four thousand mill workers here and they're going to call a strike. There's no doubt about that. What we want to know is why they're dissatisfied and who is right and who is wrong. They're sore because their wages have been cut again and because of what they claim to be a terrible stretch-out. Then there's the refusal of right to organize. All in all, they say their life is a hell on earth."

"You mean their paid organizers say so," Harriett retorted. "If the workers have complaints to make, they have their Industrial Democracy to take care of their grievances. They elect their own representatives and Papa and the rest of the officers welcome their criticisms."

"Yes, Harriett, that sounds fair enough. But the workers tell me that the overseers and lesser lights make it hot for them if they dare to criticize anything. I believe your father is fine in all his direct personal relations with the workers but—after—"

With that I stopped short, realizing that candor with the best of us only goes so far. I did not intend to speak to Harriett of her father's affliction—the acute deafness and impediment of speech—which, according to many of his critics, was making it increasingly difficult for him to know what was happening in the mills.

"These mills have been Papa's lifework. The textile industry fascinates him more than anything in the world,

just like painting fascinates me. And the labor angle has interested him most of all. He's done everything possible to
make living conditions decent in the Village. Look at the
Welfare work, the Y, the band concerts, the recreation facilities. What does the union say about all these things?"

"They say the workers had rather have the money
in their pay envelopes at the end of the week. They say it
would be better to do away with all this Welfare business
rather than cut wages again."

"Of course, they would say that. Now suppose I give
you a few facts to keep in mind before you listen to Mr.
Francis J. Gorman talk anymore."

She proceeded to give me these facts as we returned
to her automobile and drove homeward through the au-
tumn dusk. Some of her statements in defense of mill policy were startling and I tried to listen with an open mind,
hoping that we might agree in the end. In my home town
I did not have any good friends to spare and Harriett,
especially, I did not wish to lose. And in truth I knew that
her attitude toward this trouble, in spite of the fact that
she was the mill president's daughter, was remarkably
impartial: it was really a pity; I thought that she could
not have displaced some of the salaried executives to
whom all union sympathizers were Communists in need
of gallows.[196]

Tom Tippett, who also worked as a reporter, thought that
much of Danville sided with the workers. He didn't think people
thought of Fitzgerald as "the popular hero of the city, as Mr. Cone
was in Greensboro." He explained, "His father had started the mill
and made a fortune, passed it on to his son who did likewise, and
somehow or other this fact was resented generally in the town
rather than applauded. Perhaps Fitzgerald's unpopularity was due

---

196 Meade, pp. 6-8.

to somewhat physical causes. He is quite deaf and is getting old. Naturally, then, he cannot attend to all the back-slapping and other uplifting enterprises in which businessmen must indulge in these days in order to keep all their fences up. When one goes about Danville it is quite common to hear Fitzgerald criticized, not only by the working population but by the so called better element as well." Tippett imagined Fitzgerald sitting "in his office at the cotton mill, a sullen, grouchy old man, extremely disappointed in the 'unfaithfulness of his people.'"[197]

Julian Meade's brother, Robert, said that remarks against Fitzgerald and the mill were delivered in "whispers." Complaints among the middle-class citizens of Danville "were never brought into the light of day. In a Virginia county named for William Pitt, the Elder, over the border of which Patrick Henry once lived, there was a restriction upon freedom of speech," he claimed.

The local newspapers expressed the dominant ideology, which portrayed the mill dispute as a problem created by outsiders and repeated the company line. Its owner held stock in Dan River and most members of Danville's civic clubs did too, or else they worked for it or were friends with managers of the company. Although, according to Tippett, there was support for the workers, because "they made friends of other people, married into families of other trades, in some cases policemen, and in general were part and parcel of working-class life," they were seen as social inferiors by those that had power in Danville. Very few of them could vote and they had no standing in the Good Government Club.[198]

Strike!

Francis Gorman and the Dan River union local repeatedly stated that they did not want to go on strike. They simply wanted to be recognized by Fitzgerald. However, the mill's president continued to say that he would not talk with them. As spring slipped into

197 Tippett, pp. 224-225.
198 Tippett, p. 224; *Raleigh News and Observer*, August 9, 1931.

summer, production in the mill declined and workers were cut to a four-day work week. By the end of July, Dan River's board of directors met and agreed to "curtail production in all mills of the company during the next thirty or sixty days." They closed two plants and laid off two thousand mill workers, who interpreted the move not as an action necessary for the company's survival, but one carried out to break their spirit and thwart the union.

Gorman argued that Fitzgerald was trying to force the union into a strike. In a month five hundred more workers were put out of work and on September 1, 1930, the mills announced in the newspaper that they were eliminating the welfare system. Gone were the welfare department, Hylton Hall, the day-care center, and the YMCA. Fitzgerald told another mill president "in strict confidence" that he would "make a complete shutdown which will last a few weeks."[199]

Nonetheless, he started to import workers from outside of Danville to replace fired union members. Tippett believed that "the provocative actions of the mill management suggested that the company was trying to precipitate a strike in order to crush the rebellion of its workers once and for all." One union leader said that Dan River's attorney, Malcolm Harris, "repeatedly, both publicly and privately, expressed the wish that the workers would strike."[200]

The AFL and leaders of the TWUA did not want to strike. Francis Gorman and Matilda Lindsay tried to dissuade local union leaders, Buford Bash, Blackwell, and Gunn from striking, but almost all of the workers wanted to strike. On September 18, 1930, 95 percent of them voted to strike. They set September 20 as the date for the strike.[201]

After the vote Fitzgerald and his wife traveled to Charlottesville, Virginia, where they stayed with his brother to escape the pressure. Mediators from the state and federal labor

---

199 White, pp.76-79.
200 Tippett, p.221; Smith, p.317.
201 White, pp.82-83.

departments found him and tried to persuade him to negotiate. He refused.

Fitzgerald received a telegram from reporters of the Danville newspapers telling him that the strike was on. He sent them a reply stating, "If a strike has been called the mills will not open for the time being until we can ascertain what proportion of the employees are loyal to the company and desire to continue their work." He explained his actions to the stockholders in a letter, telling them that when "the situation had gotten beyond their control and even against the wishes and plans of their organizers, a strike was called, we made no attempt to check it or offer any interference... we therefore closed the gates and shut down the mills completely for several days until we could properly distinguish between those who were loyal and willing to conform themselves to an honest effort necessary to success and those who were not."[202]

Right after sending his telegram to the Danville newspapers, Fitzgerald left Charlottesville to escape reporters and stockholders. He traveled for two weeks and then returned to Danville. Union workers put up picket lines in front of the mill in his absence. A few nonunion workers showed up for work and were surprised to find the mill doors locked.[203]

The next day pickets at the Riverside Division gate stopped the plant's superintendent who had three nonunion men behind him. The superintendent, irritated by the pickets, went inside the plant and called the chief of police. The police chief declined to send any men to the plant, saying that there had been no violence and thus no cause to do so.

By noon news spread throughout Danville that two injunctions, one from Pittsylvania County Judge J. Turner Clement, and another from the Danville Corporation Court, presided by Judge Henry Leigh, had been issued on behalf of Dan River. The injunctions barred strikers from blocking the gates into the mills and ordered them to keep off of the company's property. The judges

202 Ibid., p. 90; Smith, p.317.
203 White, pp.90-92.

said that the incident involving the superintendent made their injunctions necessary. Clement said that strikers were using force and violence to "terrorize or intimidate new employees." Malcolm Harris, the company's attorney, and acting president in Fitzgerald's absence, personally wrote the injunctions for the judges. Clement owned stock in Dan River.

Two days later, on Thursday, October 2, Governor Pollard of Virginia offered to help arbitrate the strike. Fitzgerald replied, saying that there was "nothing to mediate." He said that if the governor knew of the mill's history he would know that the employees had no legitimate complaints "and if there was our employees well know that they can handle it," he wrote, "through their own committees at any time." I will "have nothing to do with these outside professional trouble makers," Fitzgerald warned.[204]

The workers longed for a settlement. A few days later President Herbert Hoover passed through Danville on his way back to Washington. Hopeful workers lined up at the train station to greet him. Meade recalled:

> When his train stopped at the Southern station he was greeted by a fair-sized crowd, who wanted a glimpse of the one man who they believed might bring the trouble to an end.
>
> The president appeared on the platform and bowed very politely for a man who was in town where Republicans suffered especial disesteem.
>
> "How's the strike getting on?"
>
> "Pretty quiet," said a striker in overalls who pushed his way to the front as a self-appointed spokesman for a group who were mostly too awed by the sight of a president in the flesh, and a Republican president at that, to have uttered a word if their lives depended upon it.
>
> "Hope it can be settled," said Herbert Hoover.

---

204 White, pp. 93-96; Smith, p. 311.

With that utterance the chief executive seemed to become more of a man, a little less distant and aloof. Our spokesman moved nearer to his superior's person, and lifted his Southern laborer's voice to tell a story of hardship and oppression inside the textile plants along the Dan. The account was tainted by a kind of bitterness, which causes immediate panic in the mind of every well-fed conservative. It was even a slightly radical account and there was no cause for surprise when the speaker was silenced by a restraining gesture of the presidential hand.

"The way to win all those things you men want is to keep the peace and not through violence," Mr. Hoover said with a tone of warning. Then he bowed again and retreated into his Pullman. What some of those workers said when he was gone could not have been repeated.[205]

Outside observers saw the strike as very orderly and quiet. According to the *Baltimore Evening Sun*, "the Danville strike, considering its importance is probably the most good-natured strike that was ever called." Julian Meade agreed: "When one thought of Gastonia it might seem that our strike was tranquil indeed."[206]

Roy Flannagan, a writer for the *Richmond News-Leader*, wrote Governor Pollard of a strange "rapport" between the union leaders and management. The unions "have firmly suppressed all individuals of the excitable radical type—will not let any known hot-heads on the picket lines, and are expelling men and women with liquor on them or in them," he wrote. Flannagan thought the strike would end immediately if Fitzgerald would recognize the union, but his "attitude now is our employees have no right to speak to us unless they speak to us through our company union (industrial democracy)."[207] Determined to destroy the union, Fitzgerald had the upper hand. The union's finances rested on

---

205 Meade, pp.43-44.
206 Mainwaring, p.292.
207 White, p.102.

shaky ground. It cost $1,000 a day to support the strikers and the union's income had come from Dan River's workers. Once the strike began this source of revenue disappeared, while relief demands increased. President Green appealed for help from the AFL, but they were of little avail. National church groups set up an Emergency Committee for Strikers' Relief, but even their aid proved to be inadequate. By mid-October the union stopped asking for aid from local businesses on the grounds that "everybody is like we are—broke." Shelves in the Danville union commissary were often bare. "The breaks in the ranks of the strikers, that is the period when large numbers of them lost hope and began returning to the mill, correspond with the times union relief was scarce," observed Tom Tippett.[208]

Three hundred to four hundred workers had gone back to work and were traveling into the mill gates in the cars of overseers. Union members traded insults with workers who crossed the picket line and went back to work. On October fifteenth, a bomb exploded in the front yard of an overseer whose testimony had been vital in obtaining the Clement injunction. The next night a black man who worked in the Riverside Division was attacked by a group of white men while a caravan of eight men abducted a white worker and took him off into the county as if they were going to lynch him. According to Julian Meade, blacks were "between the devils on both sides: they were not allowed to work and yet, as niggers among poor whites, they were looked down upon and not welcome to this union which had to upset the bare existence which gave them at least a measure of peace, if little else." He remembered, "Wild rumors spread terror: everybody heard that such and such a tragedy was on its way. People had phoned Mr. Fitzgerald that his life was in danger so I was not surprised, when I went to see Harriett one evening, to so discover that a machine gun was concealed behind the shrubbery in the front yard and that the spacious white house was well guarded by police."[209]

---

208 Tippett, p.232; Mainwaring, p.293.
209 White, p.111; Meade, p.17.

By November 21, 1930, Dan River claimed that 1,700 workers were back on the payroll. Three days later mill whistles in Schoolfield blew for the first time since the strike began. The strikers took that as a provocation. In the evening they organized a huge parade of over 2,500 people that began in the mill villages, stopping before houses of union deserters and throwing rocks and curses at the closed doors. They barricaded the main road leading to Schoolfield and blocked cars from entering the mill. Irvin Burton remembered going to work the next morning when the pickets "picked up the supervisors car and turned it around."[210]

Answering the requests of County Sheriff C. R. Murphy, Governor Pollard ordered nine hundred national guardsmen to Schoolfield. They arrived on Thanksgiving Day and stopped the picketing, burning picket tents and shelters in the process. According to Meade, Danville's upper class "breathed sighs of relief and began to talk of victory." The governor received twenty-six telegrams and letters from people in Danville thanking him, including ones from the Chamber of Commerce, the Danville Retail Merchants Association, and the Tobacco Board of Trade.[211]

The *Danville Register* printed a full-page ad by unnamed stockholders in Dan River attacking the United Textile Workers of America. Rumors spread that the company had recruited hundreds of strikebreakers from outside of the county who would come to work. In answer, around six hundred strikers marched to the mills. The police chief met them, told them to disperse, and then threw tear gas into the crowd. As the strikers ran back toward Schoolfield, the police beat forty-five stragglers and jailed them. The National Guard regiment escorted workers into the mills with bayonet-tipped rifles. The *Danville Bee_*called it "the worst disturbance since the race riots of 1883."[212]

A week later Fitzgerald announced in the Danville papers that he would now welcome back union workers. "We have no hard

---

210 Irvin Burton interview with author, July 31, 1996; Mainwaring, p.293.
211 Meade, p.42; White, p.133.
212 White, pp.142-143; *Danville Bee*, December 8, 1930.

feelings," he wrote, "toward our employees, and for most of them whom we know to be loyal at heart we have the same love as always. There is nothing to prevent them from returning to their work any day except that a lawless element have threatened and intimidated them to the extent that they fear for their lives."[213]

As he extended an olive branch in one hand he displayed an iron fist in the other. On December seventh the mill president announced the eviction of forty-seven union families from mill homes by Christmas. "It was announced in the press that furniture would be dumped into the streets on Christmas Eve," wrote Tippett. A Danville magistrate intervened and said he would not allow evictions before Christmas or at time in which a foot of snow blanketed the city. Fourteen families were evicted on December 30, 1930, and the rest on January 9. Influenza began to spread among union families, which were jammed together in four- or five-room frame houses that now had to make room for the evicted. Others, because of a poor union diet of beans, flour, and grits, with little meat, vegetables, or fruit, began to develop sores and symptoms of pellagra.[214]

At the end of the year William Green came back to Danville and said that the union would end the strike if all of its members would be allowed to go back to work without "discrimination" and if the company would agree to a committee of five arbitrators. Fitzgerald refused. Governor Pollard came into Danville to offer to mediate, but Dan River's president turned him down once again.[215]

It had long been clear that the union was losing the strike. On January 29, 1931, it came to an end with a statement by Gorman claiming that since Dan River was now taking back large numbers of union members there was no longer any reason to strike. He claimed that the company had recognized the "fundamental principle" of union membership and with the hope now that "em-

---

213 White, p.144.
214 Tippett, p.242; Mainwaring, p.297; White, p.165.
215 Mainwaring, p.398; Meade, pp.61-68.

ployer and employee" will be able to "view their problems eye to eye."[216]

Fitzgerald immediately denied that any such agreement had been made. The *Danville Register* called the strike "settlement" an "unconditional surrender of the union campaign." Meade couldn't believe Gorman. "No defeat was admitted: nothing was said," he wrote, "concerning lack of food at the commissary, the futility of struggling against the militia, the state, the public-at large. All would be well for the strikers, claimed the labor organizers as they went to their North-bound Pullmans. And they stuck to their story in spite of a stout denial from Mr. Fitzgerald—a solemn declaration that he had never ceded one point to one Union representative and never would so long as he had a breath of life."

Tippett, was incredulous too. He thought Gorman's statement made "the union appear ridiculous" and turned what could have been a "temporary defeat into a crushing disaster." In the end "some people had lost what little they had and gained nothing; but one wondered if they were more fortunate than those who, defeated in what they thought to be an effort to better their lot, were forever cowed and subdued," concluded Meade.[217]

The end of the strike seemed to be a deathblow for unions in Danville. Only a handful of diehard workers continued to hold and attend union meetings. When the AFL launched an organizational drive throughout the South and called for a general industry-wide strike in 1934 the workers at Dan River did not respond. After fifty workers from Hopewell, Virginia, came to Danville and held a union meeting, the police arrested them. The police then escorted them out of the city until they were ten miles outside of the city limits. Then a deputy stopped them, drew out his revolver, and barked, "Get yourselves outa here now an' don't cha never come back!" Proud of the town's anti-union sentiment, a Chamber of Commerce survey, published in 1940, boasted that Danville had "a body of intelligent, loyal, and stabilized type of employees, free

---

216 Tippett, p.265.
217 Tippett, pp.266-269; Meade, p.73.

from isms and labor strife." Seventy-five years after the Civil War, Danville and Schoolfield had become corporate towns; or so it seemed.[218]

The Aftermath

Just a few weeks after the strike ended President Fitzgerald died. Meade remembered:

> The last week of February I was shaken from sleep one midnight by my father who, barefooted, and clad in baggy white pajamas which made him look like a frightened ghost, stood by my bed, saying, "Get up, boy, get up quick, and write something for your papers. Harry Fitzgerald is dead."
>
> Quickly I dressed and ran down our street and around the corner to the white house, which was lighted all over and astir with activity of relatives and friends and the tradesmen of death. I got some facts for my papers: the man who had risen from office boy to the presidency of the South's largest cotton mills and the presidency of the American Cotton Manufacturers' Association had died suddenly of angina pectoris which, according to his doctors, was aggravated by the recent months of mental anguish and physical strain. When the story was telephoned to New York and Atlanta I went home and tried to sleep.
>
> There was never such mourning in Danville. Flags were at half-mast; stores closed their doors. For hours workers from the mills filed by the antique silver coffin where lay all that was left of the man whom Gorman had called their oppressor: they forgot their grudges— the big salaries and small wages, the mean boss men he

---

218 Meade, pp.291-293; Danville Chamber of Commerce, *An Industrial Survey for the Prospective Manufacture, Wholesaler, or Distributor* (1940), p.1.

had under him, the accumulation of petty grievances—
and they remembered the times he came through the
mills and called them by their names and watched them
weave and doff, the times he lent them money, the times
he found answers for personal problems they could never
have solved for themselves. They wept when a little boy,
who had been the dead man's caddy on the links came
for a last look at the golfer whose good-natured ways and
handsome tips would be sorely missed. They pooled their
resources and, even if they could not send as handsome
a wreath as a George A. Sloan or the kings of cotton,
they sent the most ornate designs their small amounts of
money could buy.

When the hearse reached the cemetery more than
a mile away the rear end of the procession of mourners
had not left the white house where the deceased had
lived and died.

The last verses of "Fight the Good Fight" had hardly
been uttered before the *Bee* was out to tell of a man who
walked "with the princes of finances but kept the common touch"; who had said, "They can kill me but they can't
scare me"; who had "proved that Napoleon was right in
saying that it is the cause and not the death the makes
the martyr." Puzzling over these oracular words before
they turned to Help Wanted or Salesman Sam, the workers who had not joined the strike told workers who had
cast their lot with the union that Almighty God would be
calling for an answer.[219]

The *Danville Register* believed that Fitzgerald's death had reunited the Danville community "in a common bond of sorrow."
It helped workers and the city's upper classes put the divisions
exposed by the strike behind them. Future works of local his-

---

219 Meade, pp. 73-75.

tory, such as Maude Clement's *The History of Pittsylvania County* and Jane Hagan's *The Story of Danville* blamed the cause of the strike on outsiders. Just like the myth of the "Danville Riot" a myth of the Danville strike, which portrayed mill workers as dupes of Northern-born labor organizers, took hold in the imagination of antiquarian historians.

According to William Mainwaring, a Danville reporter who wrote of Danville's history, the lesson they drew was the same lesson they believed that the "Danville Riot" taught: "trouble comes from the outside world: there are no grounds for conflict within the community." In reality Dan River's workers struck against the wishes of their union leaders and were practically pushed into the union by Fitzgerald's actions.[220]

The reaction to the strikers on the part of most of Danville's citizens shows how much the city changed between 1900 and 1930. When mill workers went on strike in 1902, Robert Schoolfield complained that everyone in Danville opposed the mill company and supported the workers, including the local papers. Mayor Harry Wooding spoke at union rallies and so did local city council members. When the workers struck in 1930 Mayor Wooding opposed the strikers and the whole upper-class community eventually came down on them. Sherwood Anderson stopped in Danville during the strike and addressed a crowd of union members:

> There is not any question about it. The majority of the people of this town are against you. They want you to stay by yourselves, be quiet and humble…The truth is and you know it well, they look down on you…When people look down on you, we are hurt. They take our courage away.[221]

By the end of the 1920s the ascendancy of Dan River and the Good Government Club was complete. Both represented themselves as spokesmen for the entire Danville community and were

---

220 Danville Register February 25-26, 1931; Mainwaring, pp. 305, 324.
221 Mainwaring, p. 310.

the political and social powers in the town. The workers, just like blacks in Danville, no longer voted. The Democratic Party disenfranchised almost all of the black voters and most of the white voters at the turn of the century. They no longer had any influence over local politicians in the town. While the workers of Dan River Mills were no longer considered to be citizens, but were viewed as wards of the mill who were expected to know their place and defer to their social superiors.

In return the mill workers got the benefits of Dan River's welfare programs and the benefits of white supremacy created by the Democratic Party—to have jobs that were classified as white only and to use public places that excluded blacks. When Fitzgerald seemed to renege on this contract by lowering wages and squeezing as much labor as possible out of the system he made their working conditions unbearable and his workers, in turn, organized. But the system of the mill village and welfare programs was so rigid and could function only with the total acquiescence of the workers that their organization had to be treated as a total revolt. Fitzgerald had "nothing to mediate," because he had no other choice. But the system he built and defended ended up breaking his own spirit. Its ideals were incompatible with the demands of the market and the aspirations of his employees.

CHAPTER FOUR: The Coming of the Modern South: *Danville, Virginia, and the TWUA*

A separate low-wage labor market made the South distinctive from the rest of the United States. Its farming methods, entrepreneurship class, poverty, racial segregation, and politics all were influenced by the fact that the South was, as economic historian Gavin Wright put it "a low wage region in a high wage national economy."

The distinctive Southern labor market originated with slavery, but continued after the Civil War as subsistence sharecropping dominated the agricultural market in the decades that followed. Textile plants such as Dan River Mills drew from farmers in the Piedmont and mountain areas at the turn of the century and constructed mill villages to try to attract them. However, since they lived in practical poverty before moving into the factory, textile companies were able to pay wages 30 to 50 percent less than their Northern counterparts.[222]

This created a large wage differential that appeared to be a mere example of how backward the South was compared to the North. Contemporary observers blamed this on a lack of unions in the South, a racist labor market in which whites received better jobs and social benefits over blacks and in turn supposedly deferred to upper-class elites, or simple regional ignorance, but

---

222 Gavin Wright, *Old South New South: Revolutions in the Southern Economy Since the Civil War* (Baton Rouge: Louisiana State University Press, 1986), pp.12, 130.

in reality the differences were rooted in a separate labor market that went back to the antebellum era. Efforts by Southern elites to thwart textile unions and later civil rights activists in the 1960s were in part attempts to maintain this distinctive labor market and the economic benefits and political power it accrued to them.

During World War II the Southern labor market began a process of integrating into the national market. This began with efforts by President Franklin Roosevelt and the federal government to increase wages and consumer spending in response to the Great Depression and continued during World War II with the formation of the War Labor Board, which mandated that textile companies pay higher wages and recognize unionized workers.

These changes brought a revolution to the South and to Danville in particular. During the war they were visible in higher wages and living standards in the city. In the 1950s Schoolfield village as a company town dissolved as the wage differential being paid to Danville's textile hands with those in New England converged. By the end of the 1960s the distinctive labor market had ceased to exist. Not coincidently segregation came to an end at the same time.

In just three decades the social landscape of the city evolved in ways that were unimaginable during the war. The Old South faded away. None of these things were possible without people making them happen. The South and Danville did not simply develop due to economic forces that were beyond their control. People fought to bring them about.

Franklin Roosevelt and the New Deal

In response to the Great Depression Franklin Roosevelt's New Deal created the National Industrial Recovery Act (NRA) to try to solve the problems of over-investment, saturated supply in industry and a lack of consumption among consumers. It did this by marking three billion dollars for public works spending, but more importantly it set up a government-sanctioned system of self-regulation among businesses.

NRA industry-wide codes set up production limits in order to attempt to end cutthroat competition among businesses, increase efficiency, mandate minimum wages, and limit work hours all with the goal of raising wages and profits. Section 7A of the NRA act also required that "employees shall have the right to organize and bargain collectively through representatives of their own choosing...free from the interference, restraint, or coercion of employers."

Although section 7A was a vague statement without any clear enforcement mechanism, it provided a catalyst for union organizers throughout the country, because it allowed them to portray joining unions as a patriotic act that would assist in the recovery of the economy. It also provided an enormous psychological benefit to workers who now believed that they had the support of the president behind them. Millions were inspired to write him letters in support asking for help in obtaining better working conditions.

Union membership increased throughout the country with the United Mine Workers led by John Lewis organizing the mining industry practically overnight. At the same time the Amalgamated Clothing Workers, led by Sidney Hillman, rebuilt its membership to two hundred thousand members. The United Textile Workers Union, which represented mill workers in both the North and South, saw its membership grow from fifty thousand members in 1933 to three hundred thousand in 1934.

Although thousands flocked into the textile union, the textile companies controlled the NRA board that enforced the codes in their industry. Many ignored the codes, while others forced workers to carry larger work-loads to compensate for higher wages. Working conditions for Southern textile workers worsened.

Over three hundred thousand textile workers went on strike throughout the country in 1934 in protest against the lack of enforcement of section 7A of the NRA. The leadership of the United Textile Workers Union initially opposed the strike and found themselves swept up into events. Employers used the strike to try to crush unionism, convincing governors to call the National Guard, evicting strikers from mill homes, and hiring strikebreakers.

Within three weeks the union's leadership called off the strike without consulting their members, contributing to the legacy of defeat for Southern textile workers. Although some members of the United Textile Workers Union worked in Dan River Mills, they did not organize the plant or participate in the 1934 strike. Coming so soon after the failed 1930 strike, Danville became an oasis of calm during the strike.

As the 1930s came to a close, the position of organized labor in the United States strengthened outside the Southern textile industry. The passage of the Wagner Act by Congress in 1935 created National Labor Relations Board arbitration panels to settle disputes between unions and management that gave more teeth to labor contracts. During World War II Roosevelt set up the more powerful War Labor Board to prevent and end any labor disagreements quickly in order to maintain war production. Both actions forced employers to recognize unions and listed sets of enforceable labor grievances unions and workers could file. They made section 7A of the NRA real.

Union organizers took advantage of the Wagner Act. John Lewis of the United Mined Workers and Sidney Hillman worked together to form the Congress of Industrial Organization (CIO). The group backed President Roosevelt and successfully organized the steel and auto industries, the latter under the leadership of Walter Reuther and the United Auto Workers. Sidney Hillman and labor organizers George Baldanzi and Emil Rieve also formed the Textile Workers Union of America (TWUA-CIO), a merger of the largest textile unions in the country.

The textile union successfully began organizing workers in the North with great success. However, it accomplished little in the South, winning only nine contracts in its first few years of existence. This put only 2 percent of textile spindles under a union contract in the South and meant that union would eventually have to turn southward to remain viable.[223]

The TWUA and Dan River Mills

Joe Pedigo of Roanoke, Virginia, became an organizer for the TWUA. Pedigo said his family "originally came from Patrick County in Virginia, which is way back in the mountains where you walk as far as you can walk and swing in on a grapevine, just way back in the hills. My father was a Republican and he was quite liberal and there were two things that he didn't mess with. One was his religion, he was fundamentalist Methodist and a Republican and nothing was going to change him. He never tried to dictate to us, either."

Joe Pedigo started to work in the American Viscose Corporation's Roanoke rayon mill after he graduated from high school in 1929. Rayon mills tended to pay higher wages than textile plants, because the prices for rayon products fluctuated less than those for textiles. However, "conditions were pretty bad in the 1930s," he remembered, "you could make the least mistake and there would be some little cockroach foreman that would run up to you and say, 'Look, Pedigo, if you can't do this work right, there is a barefooted boy outside looking for a job.' He was telling the truth, there was plenty of them out there looking for jobs. As far as I was concerned, if I never got anything out of a union, if I never got a raise or vacations or anything else, just to get rid of hearing that kind of stuff and be able to look the guy in the eye and speak my piece was what I was after and I think that a number of the other people were motivated by the same reason, just a question of human dignity."

Pedigo decided to start a union at American Viscose. "I recall the first meeting that we had in 1931," he said. "I slipped around thirty-five to forty people that I trusted and told them about the meeting. Not a one showed up."

---

223 American Social History Project, *Who Built America? Volume II 1877-1991* (New York: Pantheon Books, 1992), pp.351-366; Timothy Minchin, *What Do We Need a Union For?* (Chapel Hill: The University of North Carolina Press, 1997), p.14.

The workers were too scared to show up, because they feared someone from their department would recognize them and then tell management. Pedigo organized another meeting. This time he told them that they would be the only one from their shop. They'd agree to come and then he would tell the next fellow in the same shop the same thing. At the meeting "I had about twenty people, but each one of them was scared of the other ones," he said.

Before long those workers began to tell others to come to the meeting. Within a few months 800 workers out of 4,500 in the plant had joined Pedigo's union. Management got word of the organization.

One day Pedigo's foreman told him that the "front office" wanted to see him. Another man, who Pedigo recognized as the union's secretary-treasurer got called too. As they went to the office together they realized that it must be about the union. Pedigo recalled:

> We walked in the office, the plant manager was German, very abrupt, I had a lot of respect for him later on, but at the time I didn't. He didn't even invite us to sit down.
>
> He said, "What is this I hear about a union starting up down here?" I looked at this other boy and he looked at me and I decided that well, it had hit the fan now and I might as well go on with it. I said, "Well, I don't know what you've been hearing, there is a union down here, if that is what you want to know."
>
> "Why haven't they been to see me? I thought they were to bargain with management."
>
> I said, "Well, that's true, but I'll be honest with you. The reason that we haven't been able to see you was that we wanted to make sure that we had enough people in the union that if you fired us when we did come to see you, you weren't going to be able to make silk, and I'm glad you sent for us, because we are in that position now."

He went through quite a long rigmarole about why did we need a union, his office was always open and we countered by telling him that it was a pretty long way from number six spinning room to his office and by the time you got there, a telephone call would always beat you there. We had had a little experience with that.

Finally, I saw that he wasn't going to fire us and I thought. "Well, we might as well start trying to push our luck a little more," and I said, "Well look, Mr. Nerrin, the fellows are looking for me back down there in that spinning room and if I don't get back down there pretty soon, something is liable to happen and I wouldn't want that." You couldn't have pulled those people out there with a locomotive.

Pedigo said, "I've got to tell them something when I get back, so are you going to recognize us or not?"

"Of course I recognize it, there is no darn sense in the damn thing, but I recognize it," the manager replied.

After the meeting Pedigo and his friend spread the word. A few days later he rented the American Legion Hall for a union meeting. People lined up outside to join. "We organized that thing overnight," Pedigo remembered.

After several meetings with the union and plant manager the company signed a contract with the new local. It didn't specify anything in regards to wages, but it handled grievances and scheduled regular meetings between the two.

More interested in organizing instead of running the union, Pedigo soon stepped aside and let other workers take over the leadership of the union. The local affiliated itself with the TWOC and then the TWUA. Pedigo attended the first TWUA convention in 1939 where he met one of its directors, George Baldanzi. Soon afterward, Baldanzi offered him a job as a full-time organizer.

Pedigo accepted the position for $25 a week in pay. Baldanzi sent him to work in Martinsburg, West Virginia, to help a group of workers who were trying to organize a union in a mill. On his first trip he met with company management to assist the local in forming a contract with the company. The meeting seemed to go fine, as the plant manager acted cordially to him. But when he left and went to back his hotel several goons jumped out of a dark alley and tried to attack him. After the incident he started to carry a sharpened knife and made a point of making it known. He didn't have any trouble after that.

Pedigo went from place to place in North Carolina and Virginia until Baldanzi sent him to Danville, Virginia, in 1942. Wartime expansion caused a huge growth in profits for Dan Rive Mills. By the time Pedigo arrived it employed over thirteen thousand people, bringing a new wave of people to Danville just as the growth of the company at the turn of the century had done.[224]

The TWUA considered Dan River Mills a crown jewel of the South, just as the AFL did before it. However, the mill saw none of the labor turmoil that occurred throughout the region in the 1930s. At the time the failure of the 1930 strike at Dan River appeared to mark the end for unions in Danville. Over the next decade only a tiny handful of diehard union workers continued to meet about forming a new union. During the 1934 general strike in Southern textiles fifty workers came from a mill in Hopewell, Virginia, to encourage the workers at Dan River to organize to no avail.[225]

The Danville Chamber of Commerce published a survey for potential business investors in 1940. It boasted that the city had a "body of intelligent, loyal, and stabilized type of employees, free from 'isms' and labor strife." To the surprise of contemporary readers of the survey, two years later Dan River Mills would quietly become the home of the largest textile union local in the South.[226]

---

224 Transcript of interview with Joe Pedigo, April 2, 1975, *Southern Oral History Program*, E-11 (University of North Carolina, Chapel Hill).
225 Julian Meade, *I Live in Virginia* (New York: Longmans, Green, and Co., 1935), pp.291-293.
226 *An Industrial Survey for the Prospective Manufacturer, Wholesaler, or Distributor* (Danville Chamber of Commerce, 1940).

When Pedigo arrived in Danville he found that his "biggest problem" was memories of the 1930 strike, as "people really suffered." He got acquainted with some veterans of the strike, "but they were just incidental. And it would have been a mistake to have tried to gone from that reservoir anyway, it is always a mistake." Instead, Pedigo "was looking for people that other people respected and that would take a leading part in the plant on the committee," he recalled.

Sol Barken, who was the research director of the union, sent down "a whole mess of stuff as to what the background of these people were and therefore the approach should be thus and so," Pedigo said. Pedigo just put it to the side and never touched it. When Baldanzi asked if he got the stuff Pedigo told him, "Yes, for Christ's sake, if Sol wants to run this campaign let him come down here and run it, but I don't give a damn about this psychological makeup of the community or any of the sociological background or any of that stuff. I want to know what these people are saying in the pool rooms and the bowling lanes and the churches and everywhere else about this company and about what they need. When I get all that put together and get the right kind of committee, I'll have something. I won't have anything until I do."

Baldanzi let Pedigo run his own show. "So I was given a free hand, " Pedigo said, "and anybody that wanted to butt in, any of the big shots that wanted to butt in, I had an advocate that would tell them to lay off, 'these kids are running their show down there. Let them run it.' We made out all right."

Baldanzi sent down money and three others to help. "We called ourselves the Four J's. All of our initials started with J. Joel Leighton was working with me, and his wife was named Jane. Then Jennie was working...so we called ourselves the Four J's," Pedigo remembered, "Joel and I could always work together because the thing that Joel really loved to do were necessary things, but things that I despised to do."

Pedigo explained, "Joel is quite careful with bookwork, keeping a record and making sure he knew just where we stood in any given time and any given department, it was invaluable. I hated that kind of work, I always did and it went against the grain to have to do it. So, I did **99** percent of the contacts when there was just the two of us in there and Joel kept it correlated and he was a pretty good publicity man too, and we dreamed up the strategy that we were going to use."

The group ran into some trouble with the police. They wouldn't let them distribute leaflets at the gates of Dan River Mills. "I decided we had to have a test case," Pedigo recalled. "Jeannie at that time weighed about ninety pounds soaking wet and we figured she would make an appealing victim. We had it set up with cameras and everything and bondsmen all standing."

She leafleted at the gate and refused police orders to leave. Arrested, she was taken to the police chief's office. "The old police chief backed down on it," Pedigo said. "Finally he leveled his finger at me and said, 'If you are trying to get a test case you let that woman come back here one more time and you are going to get a test case.' I said, 'Well, Chief, you are doing your duty and I'm doing mine. If you get back out there in the morning, you'll get a chance to do your duty. She'll be there!' She went down on the gate and you couldn't find a policeman."[227]

The efforts of Pedigo's group quickly paid off as workers quickly signed up with the union. Soon Robert West, the president of Dan River, reported to the board of directors that "some of our workers" were "coming out in the open side of the organization drive." Several mill hands became active enough in the union to take leadership positions. Workers Douglas Eanes, a loom fixer in the mill, became president of Local 452, and F. J. Wilson, who worked as a weaver in the mills, became the secretary for the union.

By May of 1942, the union counted over half of the employees of Dan River Mills as card-signing members. The union petitioned the National Labor Relations Board (NLRB) for an election on

---

227 Joe Pedigo interview.

behalf of the workers to decide whether or not they wanted the union to represent them. The company waived its right to appeal and the NLRB scheduled an election for June 26. President Harris reported that he found the organizers doing "everything in their power to create unrest among our workers... We are still fighting in the hopes that we may find ways of at least delaying this organization. I am of the opinion that we are suffering more distress through this organization period than we would after organization, but the cost to the company is not nearly so great."[228]

An anonymous Citizen's Committee, declaring itself to be headed by local businessmen, and a Worker's Anti-CIO Association formed to oppose the union. In the weeks leading up to the election, the two groups aired radio programs and placed ads in the local newspapers. One ad in the *Danville Register* resurrected the legacy of the last strike by warning, "In 1930 an unwise decision on the part of those who were misled and deceived by the false promises of union organizers, brought upon our whole community conditions from which it took us years to recover." Irvin Burton, who drove a truck between plants for Dan River, did not think such warnings had much effect, because many of the workers in the mills were new to Danville, coming to Dan River Mills to fill jobs created by wartime expansion, or were part of a younger generation undeterred by past defeats.[229]

The organizers were also assisted by the Danville Typographical Union, composed of printers who worked for the local newspapers, which put ads in the paper countering anti-union propaganda. The ads assured readers not to fear a repetition of the 1930 strike, since it "was forced on the union because at that time it was possible for hundreds of workers to be fired without anyone doing anything about it. That does not happen now, because our government will do something about it, and mill managements know that it will." Against charges that union organizers were parasites out to collect dues and run back North,

228 Robert Sidney Smith, *Mill on the Dan* (Durham: Duke University Press, 1960), p.492.
229 *Danville Register*, June 25, 1942; Author interview with Irvin Burton, July 31, 1996.

they replied, "Don't be misled by those who call union leaders racketeers. They are performing a work for which they are better fitted than you or we. You would not call the secretaries of the Chamber of Commerce or Retail Merchants racketeers just because they draw salaries, would you?"[230]

During the election Joe Pedigo and Jennie got married. They didn't hire husband-and-wife organizing teams at the union, "but we weren't husband and wife when she went to work. We got married after she went on staff," he said. "We slipped out of Danville and went over to Reidsville and got married. She had been staying up at the Stonewall Hotel and I had been staying at the Burton Hotel just to keep talk down, you know. So after we got married, she was going to come back to the Burton and as soon as I walked back in the hotel, old lady Griffin, who ran the hotel, had a big grin on her face and said, 'I know that I'll be getting another customer now.' Everyone in Danville knew where we were going."[231]

Representatives of the NLRB supervised the June 26 election. Voting took place with secret ballots at twenty-six polling station located throughout the Riverside (in north Danville) and Schoolfield divisions of the mill. Indicating the importance they gave to voting, 12,040 out of 13,470 eligible employees cast ballots—more votes even than had been cast in any election in Danville before. One hundred and twenty of the ballots were invalid, being marked incorrectly or not all at. Of the valid ballots 7,204 were for the union and 4,716 were against it.[232]

Joe Pedigo said, "We did a pretty fair job, I think, in our approach, and the company did a magnificent organizing for us. They had really intolerable conditions there and some supervisors should have known better. We were able to capitalize on conditions."[233]

---

230 *Danville Register*, June 24, 1942.
231 Joe Pedigo interview.
232 *Danville Register*, June 27, 1942.
233 Joe Pedigo interview.

The union formed two locals: 452 and 510. One represented workers in the Riverside division of the company and the other workers in the Schoolfield division. The two locals coordinated activities through the Pittsylvania County Joint Board. However, a third local, 511—an all-black local, was formed as a result of a walkout by white workers in May 1944. Due to World War II labor shortages, Dan River Mills hired black workers as spinners and doffers in a segregated spinning room. After enough whites walked out to reduce the mills' production by 30 percent, management withdrew the blacks from "white" production jobs. Embarrassed, the TWUA national office planned to merge Local 452 and 511, but white workers' opposition to the threat of integrated employment stopped the proposal. At the time, President Harris of Dan River Mills observed that the controversy "could cause sufficient resentment among the white workers to completely crack the union here" and would mean that "both the company and the union are going to have plenty of headaches." Although segregated locals were formed as a necessary evil, they gave black union members more opportunities for leadership. Some of them would later serve as activists in the Danville civil rights movement.[234]

Jennie Pedigo served as an advisor to Local 511. "It started out as separate locals," she said. "They have only one now but they started out with a joint board. A joint board is a different structure. You set up units and each unit has so many delegates to the joint board." At times the two white locals, each of which had ten delegates, ended up vying against one another on the joint board. The four blacks representing Local 511 tended to vote together in a block, so they would often become the balance of power on the board.

"We scratched our heads over the thing," Joe Pedigo remembered, "and I still think it was the best setup we could ever make, because there were 1,300 Negroes in a plant with 13,000 workers and they would be completely lost in one unit. Here they were swinging the balance of power in the structure that we set up there...And you quickly noticed how people tended to segregate themselves in the meetings. Whites would sit in one group and the Negroes in another. It wasn't long before the whites began to realize that here was the balance of power and you'd see a white go over and sit down and put his arm around a guy's shoulder and start whispering to him"[235]

Irvin Burton, who became president of local 511, believed the union helped bring black and white workers closer together. It "built a relationship that wasn't there before the union came to town, because meeting and discussing we realize we all have the same problem," he said. The meetings on the joint board were probably the first time whites and blacks ever formally sat as equals in the same organization in Danville since the 1890s. As a result, according to Burton, these meetings created a controversy "at the beginning, because people hadn't, communities hadn't, mingled and worked together like the union advocated at." For Burton, the union meant, "getting people to believe in people. Then when you believe in people, that is mainly yourself. Cause you cannot see another person's condition until you see yourself."[236]

Black and white representatives also traveled to national union meetings together. Clyde Coleman, a black man who worked at Dan River Mills from 1939 to 1983, remembered traveling by bus to the TWUA's 1946 convention in Atlantic City with other union members. On the way to Atlantic City whites and blacks sat separately from one another. On the way back they sat together and stopped in Baltimore to eat. "They wouldn't serve us," Coleman said, "said they couldn't do it, they would serve the white in the main cafeteria, but the colored had to go to another section. So

---

235 Transcript of interview with Joe and Jennie Pedigo, April 2, 1975, *Southern Oral History Program*, E-11-2 (University of North Carolina, Chapel Hill).
236 Irvin Burton interview.

instead of eating there we went on further. If we couldn't eat together, we didn't eat separate."[237]

The Great Leap Forward in Danville

Once the union won the election it held meetings with Dan River Mills to agree to a contract. The two parties issued proposals and counterproposals back and forth. Irvin Burton recalled what being on a contract committee was like: "We didn't participate too much. They had people from the national office that did that—leading the negotiations. We would call a recess and go and discuss it among ourselves. The company run into a snag, a point that we couldn't agree on they would take a recess. See if they could come up with a language or what not that would take care of a certain proposal." The negotiators worked laboriously to create the first contract. After months of negotiating, the two sides remained far apart and the NLRB stepped in to settle their dispute. It took a whole year, but the union signed a contract with Dan River Mills.[238]

The key issues that had stalled negotiations were wages, union security, grievance machinery, and a key maintenance of membership clause in the contract. The final contract established rules for seniority and grievances. If a complaint was not settled within two days of a conference with an overseer, the matter was taken to a divisional superintendent and a representative from the local union office. If that failed it would then be taken to the company's president and a national representative of the union. Thereafter, a final appeal with an arbitrator assigned by the National War Labor Board could give a final binding decision. The contract also granted a week of vacation pay for each employee with at least a year of service. It provided payment of time and a half for holiday work and overtime in excess of forty hours a week. The contract also assigned a minimum wage of 47.5 cents per hour, short of

---

237 Minchin, p.137.
238 Irvin Burton interview; *War Labor Reports*, Vol. 8 (Washington D.C.: The Bureau of National Affairs, 1943), p.277.

the 50 cents per hour the union wanted too. All were benefits the workers had never had before.[239]

The union checkoff became the most important section of the contract. Though the company bitterly opposed it, the War Labor Board forced it to stay in the contract. The checkoff was a deduction of twenty-five cents from workers' paychecks for union dues and also required all union members to maintain their membership as a condition for employment. The board decided that it would be an "undue hardship" to require the union to "sign members all over again" if the contract did not provide a checkoff for dues.[240]

Despite the long negotiations, President Harris later described the contract signing as "somewhat of a lovefest." After the signing both sides agreed to work through any future disagreements for the mutual benefit of both sides. George Baldanzi, the TWUA vice president at the time, reassured Harris that the union's only goal was to improve the working conditions of its members and would not be able to do that if it were to "endanger" the conditions of management.

The contract should be seen as a historic event in Danville. Contemporary observers saw it as the TWUA's greatest triumph in the South, because Dan River Mills was the largest single mill operation in the nation at the time and it tended to set prices and wages for other Southern mills. During the negotiations one union member said, "Everybody is talking about what we do here. It makes us a national figure." Management agreed, believing that other mills in the industry would be watching closely to see what effect collective bargaining would have on the company.[241]

---

239 The Riverside and Dan River Cotton Mills, Incorporated and Textile Workers Union of America, Local No. 452 (CIO), Now Known as Pittsylvania County Joint Board: Contract records of Dan River Inc. personnel office (DRPO), June 25, 1943.
240 *War Labor Board Reports*, Vol. 8, p.274.
241 The Riverside and Dan River Cotton Mills, Incorporated and Textile Workers Union of America, Local No. 452 (CIO), Now Known as Pittsylvania County Joint Board: Contract records of Dan River Inc. personnel office (DRPO), June 29, 1944.

The contract signing contrasted sharply with the last attempt to organize Dan River Mills that led up to the disastrous strike in 1930. President Fitzgerald did everything he could to oppose the union back then whereas the company's management in the 1940s came to a decision to live with the union. This difference in part reflected changes inside the company. Its managers had become professional managers. The company no longer was the personal empire of one man as it had been for Harry Fitzgerald, and still was for smaller mill operators in the South. As the next few decades wore on, the largest stockholders in Dan River Mills became New York banking firms instead of individuals living in Danville or managing the company. The new professional managers proved their worth by generating dividends for their stockholders. They were willing to compromise in order to avert a strike and maintain profits.

World War II brought tremendous profits to Dan River Mills, and, as a result, it did not see compromise as endangering to its interests as smaller firms without large government contracts did. It also had a more far-sighted management. This is evident from its investments in technology and the development of new types of cloth, which set it apart from other textile operations. By the 1950s, unlike other mill companies, Dan River Mills became a multi-divisional corporation with holdings in Georgia and South Carolina.

Larry Rogin, the TWAU's educational director, credits the War Labor Board with making the key difference in the union's success, "because it took away the fear that you'd have a strike and then a company would beat the union or that you'd be fired." "The War Labor Board gave you contracts," he said. "Like we organized Dan River and we got a contract, organized Marshall Field, and there was considerably less opposition there than there had been in, say, Dan River. And the War Labor Board gave you check-off and, you know, it was the whole thing. So the War Labor Board really made the difference. But at the same time...while this was happening, let me put it that way, the employers were beginning to learn how to use the Wagner Act for delays and so on, and so organizing became rough and rougher and rougher, even while the war was on."[242]

The time of the War Labor Board in the 1940s was certainly the era of greatest union strength in Danville. According to Irvin Burton, "Most all the people were interested in the union at the time...people want improvement in working conditions and pay scale. They got wages raised, they got vacation pay, they got jury duty, and they got insurance." As the union delivered, its active membership grew thereby making it stronger.[243]

The workers used the new grievance machinery to have more say and control on the factory floor. In the last months of 1942, the company decided to revise its system of piece rates and incentive pay. President Harris noted, "For many years George Robertson," who joined the company in 1884 as head overseer of the weaving department, "handled these plants when he was unable to walk. The job-loads and rates were set up without any semblance of standardization." The company employed a consulting firm to carry out time and motion studies to determine "the amount of work produced by a normal operator working at a normal day's work speed with proper fatigue allowance in one minute." Armed with these figures the company changed its piece rate.[244]Complaining of a resurrection of the stretch-out, workers took action. Warp hangers refused to smash warps at the same pay rate as for hanging warps. The next day a group of workers in the weave room walked off their jobs, because the company had not given in to the warp hangers. One hundred more workers in the card room joined them and marched to the union headquarters. The union encouraged employees to go back to work and sent a protest to the War Labor Board.[245]

---

242 Transcript of interview with Larry Rogin, *Southern Oral History Program*, E-12 (University of North Carolina, Chapel Hill).
243 Interview with Irvin Burton.
244 Smith, p.51.
245 *Danville Register*, June 1, 1943.

The board sided with the company on grounds that technological changes were the responsibility of management. Unsatisfied, workers launched more sporadic strikes in December. The union again appealed to the War Labor Board. Although the panel ruled once again that management had the responsibility to change workloads, it recognized that such changes "give rise to problems of concern to employees." It devised a procedure to which both the company and union agreed: management first had to inform the union of any changes it decided to make; the changes would then be put on a trial period in which if the employees' earnings were less than their original average hourly rate they would be paid at the previous rate. If the union still had a grievance it had the option of filing to the board for arbitration.[246]

In 1944, the union and Dan River Mills signed a second contract that gave the workers an across-the-board raise of 2.5 cents an hour and increased paid vacations to two weeks for employees who had worked for the company at least five years. The minimum wage went up to fifty cents an hour too.[247]

During these contract negotiations, management displayed misgivings about the previous year's work stoppages. Basil Browder, the company's vice president, told union representatives, "You sign a contract that there will be no strikes, and yet you don't want to take responsibility when there is one. In this year we have had strikes and shutdowns and slowdowns, and you say you can't help that." The union countered by saying that they weren't responsible, because not all of these workers were in the union. One union member suggested that "if we could have a closed shop, then we could be responsible for what happens if the place shuts down."[248]

Two years later the union tried to win a closed shop agreement with Dan River Mills. Although several of the company's

246 Smith, pp.496-498; *War Labor Reports*, Vol. 16 (Washington, D.C.: The Bureau of National Affairs, 1944), pp. 663-666.

247 The Riverside and Dan River Cotton Mills, Incorporated and Textile Workers Union of America, Local No. 452 (CIO), Now Known as Pittsylvania County Joint Board: Contract records of Dan River Inc. personnel office (DRPO), June 25, 1944.

248 Minutes of contract negotiations, DRPO, June 17, 1944.

directors also served as directors for companies that had such an agreement, President Harris, stated that he "was determined to stand against a union shop if it means shutting down these plants for a period of months." He came to believe that he had "no more than one chance in ten of avoiding a strike."[249]

The company and the union averted a strike through compromise. The union dropped demands for a closed shop and in return Dan River Mills signed a new contract that included funds for medical insurance and an increase in the minimum wage to 73 cents an hour, eight cents above the War Labor Board's mandatory minimum at the time.[250]

In 1947 Virginia passed a right-to-work law outlawing the closed shop. Harris expressed his support for it and petitioned politicians to pass it. "The Closed Shop Contract is the most iniquitous feature of our labor relations. Even an Open Shop Contract, with the usual maintenance of membership clause, enables a small minority of militant bullies to dominate a situation in industry," he wrote one member of the Virginia House of Delegates.[251]

In 1948 the contract Dan River Mills had with the union dropped the maintenance of membership clause due to the right-to-work law, although it retained the dues checkoff. Thanks to the new contract, though, the company raised wages to an average of $1.07 an hour. According to the TWUA, this was five cents higher than the average wage in Southern textiles. In 1940, the average weekly earnings for an employee at Dan River Mills came to $38.90. Ten years later, employees took home a paycheck worth on average $124.40: more than a threefold increase.[252]

249 Smith, p. 500.

250 The Riverside and Dan River Cotton Mills, Incorporated and Textile Workers Union of America, Local No. 452 (CIO), Now Known as Pittsylvania County Joint Board: Contract records of Dan River Inc. personnel office (DRPO), June 25, 1946.

251 Smith, pp. 501-502.

252 Ibid., p. 505; The Riverside and Dan River Cotton Mills, Incorporated and Textile Workers Union of America, Local No. 452 (CIO), Now Known as Pittsylvania County Joint Board: Contract records of Dan River Inc. personnel office (DRPO), 1948.

It is hard to underestimate the impact of these wage increases on the lives of these workers and even Danville as a whole. Such pay increases made the jobs in the mill more respectable. Instead of being seen as wards of Dan River Mills by Danville's middle class, as the workers were before the 1940s, they became important consumers in the local economy, with many of them buying cars or houses for the first time.

Lester Wright remembered that there was a "stigma" attached to working for the textile company when he got his first job there as a mechanic in 1947. People saw it as a dead-end job that meant being stuck in low living conditions. Wright said this shortly changed, as wage increases and new management practices came to the forefront. Before the 1950s, the mills promoted very few employees. If it needed managers it would hire them out from other mills. This practice came to an end as the mill created night schools to train and promote from within the company.[253]

Armed with their newfound prosperity, the workers' lives and place in the Danville community were revolutionized, as they became "buyers and voters of consequence," labor writer May Heaton Vorse wrote. She had reported on the 1930 strike in Danville. In 1949 she revisited the city and found it transformed so much "that anyone who was there in the old violent days and saw how isolated from the community the workers were could hardly believe his eyes." She noticed physical changes as she saw what had been run down mill homes with overgrown yards become repainted houses owned by the workers. She found that the union hall, whose headquarters sat on Main Street, had become a symbol of prosperity and respectability for the Danville community.

The union was associated with bringing a $7.5 million increase to the annual payroll of Dan River Mills, thereby bringing more wealth to the entire community. She found union representatives helping run welfare organizations, sitting on advisory

---

253 Lester Wright, interview by author, July 1, 1996.

committees of the city and county health departments, and helping to put together the Community Chest Drive. The textile
union had become so popular that when the city's fifty bus driv-
ers joined the CIO they insisted on becoming members of the
TWUA, because, as one driver put it, "Nearly all the people we
haul are textile workers, so we want to be in the same union."
As the economic divide in Danville narrowed Vorse saw the city
as "exhibit number one" in a modernizing and more tolerant
South.[254]

Danville's political system also underwent an abrupt shift as
the union brought something not seen in Danville for decades:
workers voting. For over twenty years the Good Government
Club had depended on a small electorate and a "city hall vote"
(city employees were appointed by the city council and tended
to vote for incumbents) for its survival. Thanks in part to union
efforts, in 1946 Danville had 8,700 registered voters, a figure almost double the number in the last pre-war election. Twelve hundred blacks also registered as qualified voters. World War II had
an important impact on these figures, because Virginia exempted
veterans from the poll tax. Four hundred of the black voters were
veterans, for instance.[255]

The city council elections of 1948 demonstrated the force of
social change in Danville. The formation of two political coalitions,
the Voter's League, organized by blacks, and the union's Labor's
Legislative League, meant that once silent voices were making
their presence known in city politics. Sharing common interests,
the groups worked together and backed the same candidates. In
the Danville City Council campaign, Charles Coleman, a black
grocer, announced his candidacy and received the endorsement
of the union block. Although he lost, he was the first black candidate to run for office in Danville since Reconstruction.

254 Mary Heaton Vorse, "The South Has Changed," *Harpers Magazine* (July, 1949),
    pp. 27-33.
255 William Mainwaring, Jr., *Community in Danville, Virginia. 1880-1963*, (Ph.D. dissertation,
    The University of North Carolina at Chapel Hill, 1988), pp. 331-333.

Vernon Wilkerson, a newspaper machinist, succeeded, though, in becoming the first member of the working class to be elected to the city council since the rise of the Good Government Club in the 1920s. With only one incumbent running for re-election, the 1948 elections brought a completely new slate of city council members into power, and marked the demise of the Good Government Club, which had controlled Danville politics for over twenty-five years.[256]

These new city council members took steps to begin to diversify Danville's industrial base. No industries of any significance had moved into the city after Dan River Mills opened up. Whether true or not, a popular opinion at the time held that Dan River Mills had power over the Good Government Club and opposed industrial diversification in order to maintain a monopoly over the local labor market. A student at George Washington High School received a prize for writing an essay in 1947 which claimed that Du Pont had planned to move a plant to Danville during World War II, but was discouraged by the textile company and its local business allies. The education director of the textile union claimed that the Chamber of Commerce agreed with Dan River Mills that it was important to maintain a "good labor market" in which "there are people around out of work who will stand in line to take another man's job." A lead editorial in the *Danville Register* said it was time "to either confirm…or dispel…and, we hope for all time… the old bug-a-boo that the mills run the city council, the Chamber of Commerce, and fight tooth and to nail to keep other industry out."[257]

The city council and other civic groups succeeded in wooing other companies to Danville over the next several decades. In 1959, Diston, a saw and tool manufacturer, opened a plant in Danville. Corning Glass then followed in 1960 and a massive Goodyear tire plant came in the mid-1960s.[258]

---

256 *Danville Register*, June 1, 3, 9, 12, 1948.

257 *Danville Register*, January 26, 1947; Smith, p.470.

258 Malcolm Cross, *Dan River Runs Deep: An Informal History of a Major Textile Company, 1950-1981* (New York: The Total Book, 1982), p.98.

The new city council immediately resurrected what had been a taboo issue for decades: the annexation of Schoolfield Village. Dan River Mills opposed annexation on the grounds that it would increase its tax burden and thereby pose "an economic menace to the entire southside area." Nevertheless, on July 1, 1951, Danville annexed Schoolfield, adding 15.75 miles and eleven thousand people to itself.[259]

Immediately after annexation the company decided to sell all of its "village houses" to its employees, thereby ending the last vestige of the paternalistic experiment begun by Dan River Mills and Harry Fitzgerald at the turn of the century. As the workers earned more money the mill homes no longer served any purpose for the company. Most of the workers now drove cars to work. Others had simply purchased their own homes outside of the village. As Malcolm Cross, the industrial relations director for Dan River Mills, put it, "the mill village had become an anachronism."[260]

Schoolfield, now no longer a mill village, became just another neighborhood in Danville. Symbolically, the mill's shift whistle, whose sound had blanketed the town for years, was taken down and placed in one of the offices at Dan River Mills and put on display as a historical artifact. Most Schoolfield residents welcomed annexation. It came to represent all of the changes that had taken place in their lives due to their newfound prosperity and rise in social status. According to David Ray Handy, one resident of Schoolfield:

There was a time that Schoolfield was looked down on a little from people downtown, but that didn't last. I can remember that. I can remember that there was people that lived downtown that showed that they felt like that they was up a little. But it didn't take us long to put them down. For them to get down there with us. That's when

---

259 Mainwaring, pp. 339-341; Cross, p.9.
260 Cross, pp.6-7.

we really accomplished what we started out to do—
to have a community that there weren't no ups or
downs.[261]

World War II prosperity, unionization, and the new respect
for textile workers demonstrated that Danville was becoming
a more open community. As William Mainwaring, who wrote a
history dissertation on Danville, noted, "Although it is doubtful
that Danville's upper middle class considered textile workers as
equals, by 1949 it could no longer dismiss them as lintheads."[262]

The Strike of 1951

Although the textile union had a powerful role in Danville, most
Southern textile communities remained unorganized after World
War II, in contrast with a heavy TWUA presence in Northern
textiles. The union boasted a national membership of four hundred thousand workers. However they counted 85 percent of the
textile workers in the New England and Mid-Atlantic states organized and only 20 percent in the South. Southern textile plants
paid lower wages than Northern plants, causing many of them
to shut down or move their operations to the nonunion South,
thereby threatening the union's membership base.[263]

It became important for the TWUA to raise wages in the
South to protect the Northern textile companies, where most of
their members worked. During World War II, TWUA President
Emil Rieve lobbied the War Labor Board to raise the minimum
wage for textile workers by demonstrating that Southern wages were "substandard." These efforts culminated in several War

---

261 David Handy interview, Tape F, "Schoolfield Virginia—Life in a Mill Village (1903-
    1951)." *An Oral History Documentation Project Sponsored by the Virginia Foundation for the
    Humanities and Public Policy and Averett College.* Quoted in Mainwaring, p.404.
262 Mainwaring, p.342.
263 Clete Daniel, *Culture of Misfortune: An Interpretive History of Textile Unionism in the
    United States,* (Ithaca: Cornell University Press, 2001), pp.155-157.

Labor Board mandated wage increases at Dan River Mills and other textile plants in the South.[264]

These wage increases still weren't enough to rectify the wage disparity between Northern and Southern mills. After World War II came to an end a postwar slump in the textile market began a decline in the New England textile industry, which continued uninterrupted until none were left by the end of the century. Thirty-seven New England Mills closed their doors in 1949. By the middle of 1949 the TWUA calculated that 250,000 workers were unemployed in the New England states. In New Bedford unemployment rates among textile workers reached 40 percent. Leading Northern manufacturers blamed their woes on their competitors to the South.[265]

Emil Rieve, and his staff, decided that something had to be done to close the wage differential between the Northern and Southern textile mills. An editorial in *Textile Labor*, the TWUA's magazine, stated, "It is better to face the facts than gloss them over. Our only present alternative would be industry-wide strikes, many in violation of contracts, which might well wreck the union, the organized segment of the industry, or both." Once contract negotiations opened up in 1951, with Dan River Mills and several other key textile plants in the South, Rieve decided to try to win a 10 percent wage increase in these plants.[266]

Rieve saw Danville as a key to his campaign, because as Julius Fry, a negotiator for the TWUA put it, "we had good organization and union contracts with Dan River Mills, the Cone Mills Corporation, and Fieldcrest, or Marshall Field, I believe it was then. And Erwin Mills, Durham, Erwin, and Cullowhee, we had all of them. And at one time, we even had little Erwin Mill in Stonewall, Mississippi. And we would set industry wage patterns, by bargaining with Cone, Dan River and Fieldcrest and Erwin, just in that little triumvirate, we would reach an agreement with them by

---

264 Minchin, p.15.
265 Ibid., p.102; Daniel, p.207.
266 Daniel, p. 213

working with the locals, and they would work together too, and we would set the pattern for the industry." Management at Dan River Mills saw things the same way. "When Dan River set a pattern," one management official said, "as it has in the past on some occasions, of course, these mills in the areas usually follow."[267]

Not all in the union supported Rieve's plan. Emanuel Boggs, the head of the Danville union's joint board, warned that if they had to strike, "we'll get our membership and a little more for a week and after that they'll start going back." Other Southern organizers also thought a strike would fail, but feared being called "a bunch of creampuffs" by Rieve supporters if they spoke up. Some in the union thought Rieve was using the situation in order to keep control of the union and displace loyalists of George Baldanzi, who had built up a large enough following to threaten Rieve for leadership of the TWUA. An open rift had developed between supporters of the two inside the union.[268]

The union sent a contract proposal to Dan River Mills including demands for higher wages, greater benefits, and adjustments for cost of living increases, attached to a warning that it would go on strike if they weren't met. The company calculated that they would cost it $12.5 million.

Negotiations between Dan River Mills and the union began on February 27, 1951. After several weeks of discussions the two parties remained far apart. On March 15, the TWUA succeeded in signing new agreements with its Northern mills, but could not get any with its Southern mills. A week later Emil Rieve decided to personally take charge of the negotiations in Danville, pushing aside George Baldanzi who had led the negotiations in the past.

He told the management of Dan River Mills that the union couldn't afford not to sign a new agreement with one of its Southern textile plants and would strike if necessary. Basil

267 Transcript of interview with Larry Julius Fry, Southern Oral History Program, E-4 (University of North Carolina, Chapel Hill); minutes of negotiations between Dan River Inc. and TWUA, DRPO, March 21, 1951.
268 Daniel, p.216.

Browder, who headed the company's side of the negotiations, said that the company could not meet Rieve's demands and still compete with other Southern mills, because "you have got better than 80 percent that is not organized that we are having to compete against. Now, when you get all those folks lined up here and doing as well as Dan River does, then we would be able to talk to you about doing more." The union's small base in the South guaranteed that an industry-wide strike would have great difficulty in succeeding.[269]

The TWUA's negotiating tactics upset the management of Dan River Mills. They did not like the fact that the union issued an ultimatum to them. The company thought it had built of up a solid relationship with the union and claimed that its leadership was jeopardizing it for the sake of union politics.

Emil Rieve also was new to negotiating in the South. Browder and his team thought he had a brash negotiating style and at times was overbearing. According to Malcolm Cross, in contrast with Baldanzi, "he was not necessarily liked by mill managements of the South." Some blamed him personally for the impasse. Emanuel Boggs thought "Rieve was never able to communicate effectively in the South. He had this thick accent and brusque personality that made it extremely difficult for him to understand Southerners or for Southerners to understand him."[270]

Unable to reach an agreement the workers at Dan River Mills walked out on April 2, 1951. According to Larry Rogin, the education director for the TWUA during this time, "The '51 strike, there is a question of whether that strike would have taken place if it hadn't been for the conflict in the union. And I don't know whether it would have or not; it's very hard to say. But there is no question that the northern employers were beginning to say, 'We won't raise wages anymore first; you've got to get them up in the South first.' Or, 'We'll do it this time and won't do it again.'"

269 Minutes of negotiations between Dan River Inc. and TWUA, DRPO, March 21, 1591.
270 Cross, pp. 14-15; Minchin, p. 126.

Rogin continued, "The pattern had been we were better organized in the North, we negotiated an increase in the North. Then you went South into the unionized mills and you made a pass at organizing widely—you know, have what you call a wage increase drive, and you'd negotiate. But the northern mills were getting tired of this, because you never negotiated quite as much in the South as you did in the North: the fringe benefits weren't as good, and so on. So the union was going to have to find out whether it could move these plants that had been organized in the war (there's Cone and the ones in Gadsden and Danville and Huntsville, and so on, and Rock Hill, of course, in the big finishing plant there, and the others). And at some point, I think, the same thing would have had to be done. But I think that the internal fight in the union prevented people from telling honestly what they thought would happen when the strike was called...the only one we got a real honest statement of it was a Baldanzi supporter in Dan River Mills. He said what would happen, and it did."[271]

The company decided to fight the strike to win. It announced in the *Danville Bee* that "the strike can end either of two ways—by employees coming back to work on their own, or by a vote to rescind the strike call." As a harbinger of things to come, an editorial in the *Danville Commercial Appeal* said:

> The extension plans being made and carried out by Dan River clearly shows "this is it" as far as the company is concerned; in other words this is the showdown. The textile industry is in a letdown since the war and from the standpoint of supply and demand, the calling of the strike seems most untimely—that is from the union's standpoint...It is a mistake, we think, for Danville to rejoice at the prospect of a union defeat in the strike. We fear that it may mean a union defeat, period. Good done by the union for the workers is obvious.[272]

---

271 Rogin interview.
272 *Danville Bee*, April 6, 1951; *Danville Commercial Appeal*, April 13, 1951.

The day after the strike began the company kept its plants running and 22 percent of its workers showed up for work. The union had a difficult time ahead. "In retrospect the strike was fought on three fronts," Malcolm Cross wrote. The most important of these was the picket line. If enough workers went back to work then the strike would collapse. Secondly, the union and the company used the newspapers and airwaves to try to get their respective messages out to the community. Lastly, some workers transferred their anger over the strike into violence. The act of workers crossing the picket line generated strong emotions among the strikers.[273]

As the strike continued, tensions increased. Kathryn Watson, who came to the mill in 1947 and worked as a clothing inspector before she was transferred to the clerical department, recalled sending her son out of town to live with her mother during the strike. On the second day of the strike she went back to work and experienced the wrath of friends who called her a scab, even though she was not allowed to join the union, because she held an office job. "They didn't know what a scab was, I wasn't a scab. A scab is someone who takes someone else's job," she said.[274]

The strikers established a twenty-four-hour picket line. Irvin Burton remembered manning it and watching some workers drive through the gates with sheets over their heads. The company took out all the stops to defeat the union pickets. Malcolm Cross wrote, "Intelligence activities frequently alerted management as to where the pickets would be concentrated on a given shift. Cars were naturally diverted to other gates. At the end of the shift, traffic control within the mill lot would direct the cars out of the gate with the fewest incidents." The company eventually bypassed the picketed entrances by constructing a walkway above them that led from the workplace into a parking lot across

---

273 Dan River, Inc., employment figures, DRPO, April–May, 1951; Cross, p. 18.
274 Kathryn Watson interview by author, July 2, 1996.

the street. Some strike-breaking workers simply slept inside the plant.[275]

Dan River Mills also hired a New York public relations firm, Fisher and Rudge, Inc., to help plan their strike campaign. The company placed announcements in local newspapers favorably comparing their wages to those of other Southern textile mills and pointing out its need to keep costs low to meet competition. Both the textile union and the company aired radio broadcasts. Malcolm Cross believed that the company's broadcasts were more effective, because they were hosted by men who were already well known in the community and had "obvious Southside Virginia accents" when compared to the Northern voices the union aired.[276]

The company tried to attack the union by claiming that the strike was unpatriotic since 1 percent of the orders at Dan River Mills were marked for use in the Korean War. An editorial in the *Danville Bee* followed the company line by asking, "One wonders how the individual unionist who had a son or brother with the armed forces today" feels about striking against war production? Likewise, the state commander of the American Legion and Mayor Curtis Bishop issued statements fingering the Reverend Charles Webber, a TWUA organizer who came to Danville to assist in the strike and was often heard on the union's radio spots, as being a Communist.[277]

The union countered these charges by claiming that Dan River Mills was really the unpatriotic one. A union broadcast said, "Our boys are in Korea, fighting against a Communist dictator, they are battling and dying there, but Dan River Mills hasn't suffered. The Korean War has been very profitable to them. While our boys are fighting and dying, Dan River Mills's net profits have gone up 249 percent!"[278]

---

275 Irvin Burton interview, Cross, p. 19.
276 Cross, p. 20.
277 *Danville Bee*, April 12, 1951; Union strike bulletin, DRPO, April 23, 1951.
278 Transcript of union broadcast, DRPO.

Despite the company's rhetoric, veteran employees were more receptive to the union's message than civilians. Company records show that veterans were among the last to come back to work. Toward the end of the strike, on April 24, around 63 percent of the workers had come back work while only 41 percent of the veterans had. Blacks were also among the last to cross the picket line. Irvin Burton believed that one reason for this was because the union brought benefits to black workers that they never had before, such as insurance.[279]

Each side tried to claim that the other was employing "outsiders" to try to win the strike. The mill leaked news to the Danville newspaper that a red-haired "mystery woman" was leading the strikers on the picket line. On April 18, the *Danville Register*, placed a photograph of her on their front page and ran a story asking who she was and where she came from. The next day, the union answered in a radio broadcast that her name was Lillian Yadon and that she was well known to "thousands of strikers." The union charged that the talk of a mystery woman had been propaganda created by the Fisher and Rudge firm whose offices were on Park Avenue in New York City.[280]

Some of the workers went beyond the use of words and resorted to violence. The Danville police department found itself swamped with vandalism complaints, the most common being punctured tires. The first serious act of personal violence was the stabbing of Willie Davis Shirley after he got into an argument with another worker over the strike.[281]

Dynamite explosions rocked the town. King Glaise, who went to work despite the strike, found a bundle of material burning beneath his home. He quickly picked it up and tossed it away. It then hit a wire fence and exploded, damaging a neighbor's home. He ran to his brother's house and found another stick of dynamite that turned out to be a dud. A week later an-

279 Dan River Inc. employment figures, DRPO; Irvin Burton interview.
280 Transcript of union broadcast, DRPO, April 19, 1951.
281 "Danville police report complaints," DRPO; *Danville Register*, April 7, 1951.

other explosion inside a manhole plunged all of Schoolfield into darkness for half an hour. Ironically, the Schoolfield plant, using emergency generators, remained the only building lit during the blackout.[282]

Both the union and the company deplored violence. Before the strike began, management held a meeting with its supervisors and told them that all violence would be discouraged and to exercise caution around the factory gates. Nonetheless, one of the ugliest incidents took place on the company's doorstep.

On the morning of April 16, some Dan River Mills personnel connected hoses to the fire hydrants near the gates. When a picket asked one of these men what they were doing he responded, "Be there at midnight and you will soon find out." During the afternoon shift change, workers leaving the mill taunted the pickets. "Bring bathing suits tonight," one exclaimed. After the union complained, a spokesman for the company claimed they hooked up the hoses for a "routine inspection."[283]

The next day an overseer drove by the picket line in his car and fired shots into the crowd. One bullet passed through one striker's hat and another cut a union member's cheek. In response, the strikers became more aggressive. They laid themselves down in the road and tried to block the traffic. State police lobbed tear gas into the pickets and dispersed them. Two strikers had to be taken to the hospital after the fleeing crowd trampled one while a tear gas canister hit another.

The company blamed the incident on union agitators from "outside our community." The union claimed the company tried to provoke an incident that "would lead to violence." It is very doubtful that Dan River Mills encouraged the overseer's actions. One union coordinator described him "as a hot-headed person who loses his temper easily."[284]

---

282 *Danville Bee*, April 19, 1951; *Danville Register*, April 26, 1951.
283 Notes of meeting between management and supervisors, DRPO, March 13, 1951; transcript of union radio broadcast, DRPO, April, 1951; the *Bee*, April 17, 1951.
284 *Danville Bee*, April 17, 1951.

Nevertheless, the company increased tensions along the picket line by threatening strikers with fire hoses. The *Bee*, which supported the company throughout the strike, blamed the union. Despite the support the union had with the workers and their integration into the Danville community segments of the community opposed the union. Both of the city's two main newspapers opposed the strike and focused their attention on its violence instead of the actual issues of dispute between the company and the union.

The union had hopes that the government would intervene and settle the strike. President Truman had established a Disputes Section of the Wage Stabilization Board that could arbitrate the strike. The union offered to end the strike and submit their demands to this board. Convinced that it was winning the strike, the company rejected their offer. The union's attempt to use the federal government for help demonstrates how its position had weakened since World War II. During the war, it had been dependent upon the War Labor Board to even get Dan River Mills to sign a contract. With the war over and the board disbanded the union's power was precarious.[285]

On May 5, the union voted to end the strike and return to work. The union lost the strike in Danville simply because it was unable to keep its members from crossing the picket line for two main reasons. Thanks to the wage increases of the 1940s, many of the workers were able to buy homes, cars, and expensive consumer appliances for the first time. Many of these items were paid for by loan or credit. The union provided only groceries for strike relief and many of the workers were afraid to take any chances on their payments. Thus they felt compelled by economics to go back to work.[286]

Norris Tibbetts, who served as a business agent for the Danville local and headed the union relief effort, found the union's support of the strikers inadequate. In line with past strikes, the

---

285 *Danville Bee*, April 21, 1951.
286 This thesis is articulated in Minchin.

union handed out food relief, but workers needed money to meet their debts. In the first days of the strike he noted that the strikers who were "paid yesterday and now have emergency. Won't lose cars, furniture, or homes. Several people have torn up their cards and said they are going back to work." So many of them were on credit that they "can't get along—not even for a week." He saw many union members cross the picket line weeping. "What can you say to them? You weep with them," Tibbetts wrote.

"Dan River workers were by no means well off but they were just beginning to get something to lose, a car, a refrigerator, payment on a house," Tibbetts remembered. Between 1941 and 1951 their wages had increased 201.3 percent, while wages of other textile workers in the South rose on average 151.3 percent. "The union helped bring it about," Tibbetts thought, "but how can you lean on these people to the point of saying 'you have to give up everything you've gained in eight years under the union in order to pick up another couple of cents an hour'?"

Dan River Mills increased the pressure by using its influence in Danville against the strikers. In other mills the TWUA struck at the time the factories shut down. Banks and lending companies in these communities gave grace periods for debts. Louis Hathock, who led a TWUA strike in Alabama, said that "on the debts the merchants have told us, 'You people, forget your debts until after the strike. After that, start back paying.'" In contrast, in Danville, George Baldanzi, found "a complete organization of the community against the union. There was a complete cut off of credit. The company public relations agency had lined up every bank, and every credit agency in town...What we have there is a concentrated attempt to break the union beyond anything in my experience." [287]

Finally, the mill also turned the screws on the strikers by hiring new workers. Other textile mills that were struck by the TWUA in the area shut down operations, thereby freeing up

---

287 Minchin, pp. 142-148.

their labor pool to work at Dan River Mills, which was leading the fight for the industry in the strike. The TWUA claimed that other textile companies were importing strike breakers to the company. For instance, Fieldcrest Mills, which was a short drive from Danville in North Carolina, shut down operations during the strike. Supervisors from Dan River Mills visited Fieldcrest workers' homes and recruited them. Other workers received letters offering work in Danville. Some mistakenly thought that they had an opportunity for a full-time job, but once the strike ended the textile company hired back its union members due to their contract. Nevertheless, many of the strikers feared that their jobs might be permanently taken from them. "That was used as a whip to fool a lot of people and scared some," Irvin Burton recalled.[288]

The TWUA not only lost in Danville, but throughout the South. With less than 20 percent of the workers in the Southern textile industry unionized, it had little chance of successfully launching an industry-wide strike. Its only hope was to get a group of large price-setting firms, of which Dan River was a part, to agree to its wage increases, but its very position in the South made these companies unwilling to do so. In the end the strike devastated the TWUA. Its membership base in New England dwindled as Northern textile plants poured into the nonunion, low-wage South.

In Danville, the strike harmed the relationship the union had with its members and the community. According to Irvin Burton, "If you have a union, you have a few thousand people to vote for improved conditions, and you fail to live up to that, then that destroys the relationship with a lot of people. Not only people who work in the mills, but people who look for support, by exchanging merchandise and what from furniture stores, the banks, and what not. It affects the whole town."[289]

After the strike, George Baldanzi, the vice president of the TWUA, led an open revolt against Emil Rieve. Baldanzi broke away from the TWUA-CIO and became president of the United

---

288 *Textile Labor*, May 5, 1951, Irvin Burton interview with author August, 24, 1996.
289 Ibid.

Textile Workers, which was affiliated with the AFL. Many of the top TWUA union organizers in the South joined him, including Joel Leighton. Joe Pedigo stayed with the TWUA, but soon got fired for his associations with Baldanzi and other unionists who left the TWUA. Baldanzi came to Danville and petitioned for the NLRB to grant a new election. Leaders of the local union supported him.[290]

The election took place on October 30, 1952. The voters had three choices: to vote for the TWUA-CIO, the UTW-AFL, or for no union at all. Dan River Mills launched a campaign to encourage the latter. It sent letters to employees asking, "Have you any assurances that either union will lead you any more wisely now than in 1951, when you were called out to strike?" According to Malcolm Cross, the company tried "to isolate workers from the union meetings... The unions could not communicate effectively with workers on the job; therefore, their major contact had to be at off-hour meetings. The tactical approach to dissuade workers from attending union meetings was to keep them occupied with other diversions in their free hours." Therefore, the company expanded its recreation program and provided religious revival programs for its workers.[291]

Baldanzi's UTW-AFL won the election despite the anti-union campaign. His group received 7,689 votes while the TWUA received only 278 votes. Only 1,624 workers voted for no union at all. Workers voted for the UTW, not so much due to dissatisfaction with Rieve, but because they were more familiar with Baldanzi. Rieve had visited Danville only twice since the first TWUA election while Baldanzi had come multiple times. He helped during the union's first election drive and repeatedly delivered memorable speeches to the workers. Irvin Burton recalled that "he was an orator. He could rise you up off your feet... he was classified at that day as one of the best orators in the community."[292]

---

290 *Danville Bee*, July 21, 1951; Pedigo interview.
291 Basil Browder letter to all employees, DRPO, October 27, 1952; Cross p.26.
292 Cross, p.26; Irvin Burton interview, August 24, 1996.

The UTW signed its first contract with the company in August of 1953. The union, already weakened by the strike, received a huge blow when the company refused to include the dues check-off in the new contract. The loss of the checkoff meant that the union could no longer receive deductions from paychecks of union members. Malcolm Cross thought "a weak union is better than no union," because "the nature of Dan River operations is such that it always be attractive to unions. We would constantly be harassed by organizations attempting to unionize our employ-ees, and who may be more militant if they are successful."[293]

The union never recovered from the loss of the checkoff. With shrinking dues and a smaller and less-active membership the union became increasingly ineffective. A union bulletin in 1966 said, "Union means fighting for a better tomorrow; not crying over the disappointment of yesterday." The union tried to regain its strength by attempting to bring back the checkoff with another strike in 1974, but it quickly failed.[294]

The union became so impotent that Hattie Landrum believed that after it lost the strike in 1951, which she stayed out of for its duration, the union represented the company. In the 1970s Dan River Mills changed the type of cloth her machine was using. The new cloth was tougher and she could no longer make an adequate piece rate. Her work section went to a steward to complain, but he said that the union was unable to do anything.[295]

After the 1951 strike the union also disbanded the Labor's Legislative League, meaning that no labor group would speak for the interests of the working class in Danville politics any longer. During the 1960s, the Danville civil rights movement overshad-owed unionism. Blacks eventually won integrated job employ-ment at Dan River Mills through civil rights lawsuits against the company that weren't supported by the union. Emanuel Boggs thought the 1951 strike "set the economic movement in the tex-

293 Cross, p.34; Minchin, p.150.
294 Union bulletin, DRPO, 1966; Cross, pp.173-174.
295 Hattie Landrum, interview by author, August 13, 1996.

tile industry back to the extent that no progress has been made in the South since that fatal strike, and economic losses have resulted in the New England area."

Tibbetts learned a great deal from the strike. "We have made many mistakes," he wrote. "We made our first mistake in trying to make noises like an industry-wide union, which we are not. We have about 15 percent organization in the South. A solid strike among what we have organized would affect only 10 percent of the cotton industry...Who the hell are we to act like the UAW and GM?"[296]

Despite the virtual disappearance of the union after the strike, it left its mark on Danville. Wartime prosperity and organization brought unheard of prosperity to workers at Dan River Mills and helped to integrate them into the rest of the Danville community. The eye of corporate paternalism in Schoolfield village became an artifact of the past. The Labor's Legislative League also made their voices heard in local politics.

Likewise, the union demonstrated to its members the possibilities of organization and provided a training ground for a generation of activists, some of whom became leaders of the civil rights movement in Danville. In sum, it helped make Danville a more open community.

Nevertheless, most of the history of the union—not only its defeats, but its accomplishments—has been left out of Danville's historical memory. When a textile strike is referenced people in Danville usually think back to the strike in 1931 or combine the 1931 and 1951 strikes together into one memory.

As Irvin Burton noted, "As the years go on, the memory of a strike goes with time. And when time's up against us you gotta start all over...you have a new generation and you can't find too many youngsters who compare the history of the past with the history of today. Until people observe what is being done for the benefit of the community I don't know how you can stop that." There have always been people who have made an impact on the

296 Minchin, pp. 117, 153.

history of Danville, with some generations passing on a life of activism to their descendants, but without a knowledge of that it is hard for some people to imagine that they can make a difference themselves in the community if they want to, or even accomplish anything for themselves.[297]

---

297 Irvin Burton interview, August 24, 1996.

CHAPTER FIVE: Virginia in the 1940s

With the organization of the TWUA-CIO, increased wages for workers at Dan River Mills, and the exit of the Good Government Club from city politics, we can look back today on the history of Danville and see the 1940s a time of momentous evolution for the city and the South. They marked the beginning of the end of a distinctive separate labor market in the region and would lead to the civil rights movement in the 1960s and the end of segregation.

However, for people alive at the time it wasn't always easy to perceive the magnitude of the changes that were taking place, to understand them, much less to predict where they would lead. It's always easier to understand such things when looking back upon them. Hindsight, however, can also lead one to see the past as an inevitable chain of events. They weren't and people alive back then certainly didn't see them as so.

Although Virginia's economy grew rapidly during World War II, many things at the time seemed like they would never change. The state still had a poll tax, racial segregation, and remained under the rule of a Democratic political machine that had existed since the end of Reconstruction and the Danville "riot." Virginia's political elites did perceive the importance of the social changes taking place and felt threatened by them.

The Byrd Machine

Political scientist V. O. Key, Jr., in his classic 1949 book *Southern Politics in State and Nation*, described Virginia as the state most thoroughly controlled by an oligarchy in the American union. A faction within the Democratic Party, headed by Harry Flood Byrd, dominated Virginia's political system for much of the twentieth century. The most powerful politician in Virginia, from 1915 to 1965, Byrd held various political offices in the state, including Virginia governor and senator. Much of his power was owed to an efficient handling of a restricted electorate.[298]

In order to register to vote, a Virginian citizen had to pay three years' worth of a poll tax, a fee of $1.50 per year, fill out a written application with the registrar, and have the ability to answer any questions the registrar may have "affecting his qualifications as an elector." The poll tax, however, had to be paid at least six months before the general election, long before any interest in the primary took hold in Virginia. On average between 1925 and 1945 only 11.5 percent of the adult population voted in Virginia's elections.[299]

The tax had the effect of keeping most blacks and poor whites away from the voting booths. This was intentional. As Carter Glass, who helped write the poll tax, explained, "Discrimination! Why that is precisely what we propose; that is exactly what this convention was elected for," during a debate over its passage. The tax had an immediate effect on the size of the electorate. In 1900, 264,240 Virginians cast ballots for president. Four years later, after the poll tax became a part of the Virginia Constitution, only 135,867 did so.[300]

With a small electorate, the Byrd organization had to win the support of only 5 to 7 percent of the adult population to win the Democratic nomination and put its candidate into the governor's mansion. The poll tax and the repeated string of victories that the Byrd organization won had important psychological effects,

298 V. O. Key, Jr., *Southern Politics in State and Nation*, (Knoxville: University of Tennessee Press, 1996) pp.19-20.

299 Robert Gooch, *The Poll Tax in Virginia Suffrage History: A Premature Proposal for Reform (1941)* (Charlottesville: Institute of Government, University of Virginia, 1969), pp.12-14.

300 Ibid., p.5; C. Van Woodward, *Origins of the New South: 1877-1913* (Louisiana: Louisiana State University Press, 1995), p.333.

which helped to encourage voter apathy. Robert Whitehead, an opponent of the organization, noted that "much of the power of the Byrd machine is based on its reputation for invincibility."[301]

Not surprisingly, a survey of Virginia voting behavior done by the *Richmond Times-Dispatch* in 1946 found that many adults had never cast a ballot. When asked why she didn't vote, one woman from Lynchburg responded that "elections are a foregone conclusion." People repeatedly told the paper that they "just never thought much about elections." Francis Miller, who ran for governor in 1949, remembered asking a painter in his neighborhood whom he had voted for. "Colonel," he replied, "you know I don't belong to the folks who vote." Most Virginians thought of politics as a caste affair, reserved only for the elite.[302]

Hierarchy characterized social and political life in Virginia. One *Washington Post* reporter commented that Virginia had a "government of the gentry, by the gentry, and for the gentry—with the gentry's dutiful awareness that it has an obligation to keep the common people happy." Harry Byrd, a descendant of William Byrd, one of the most important men in the development of colonial Virginia, himself embodied a Virginia tradition of aristocracy and paternalism. Owning one of the largest apple orchards in the world he was a renowned and wealthy businessman. One biographer of Byrd wrote, "Like plantation owners of the antebellum South, Byrd lived the code of the gentleman, giving no offense but quick to take offense."[303]

Harry Byrd described himself as a progressive dedicated to fiscal conservatism and a definition of liberty as "freedom restrained by responsible self-government." Throughout his career

---

301 Key, 19; J. Harvie Wilkinson III, *Harry Byrd and the Changing Face of Virginia Politics: 1945-1966* (Charlottesville: The University Press of Virginia, 1968), p.37; *Washington Post*, June 19, 1957, p.A-15.

302 *Richmond Times-Dispatch*, May 12, 1946 (Meade's survey includes four articles: March 31, May 12, July 7, August 4, 1946); see *Washington Post*, June 11, 1957, for Miller quote.

303 Ibid., Richard Cope, "The Frustration of Harry Byrd," *The Reporter* (November 21, 1950), pp.21-25; Ronald Heinemann, *Harry Byrd of Virginia* (Charlottesville: University Press of Virginia, 1996), p.289.

he consistently claimed that the state government should uphold its honor, keep order, safeguard property, defend states' rights, and maintain a small and balanced budget. Reflecting Byrd's disgust for budget deficits, "a pay-as-you-go" highway construction program, financed by gas and licensing taxes instead of bonds, was one of the legacies he gave Virginia for which he was most proud. To him it symbolized his fiscal conservative philosophy.[304]

As boss of Virginia's most powerful political organization, Byrd served as the State's governor and its most senior senator until the 1960s. Commenting in 1958, Governor Lindsay Almond, Jr., described the Byrd machine "as a club, except that it has no bylaws, constitution, or dues. It's a loosely knit association, you might say, between men who share the philosophy of Senator Byrd." Harry Byrd said, "We are a loose organization of friends, who believe in the same principles of government."[305]

The Byrd machine did not act as a centralized authority, but as an informally organized group whose power rested in county courthouses throughout the state of Virginia. Each county served as home to five elected administrative officials: commonwealth's attorney, treasurer, commissioner of revenue, clerk of court, and sheriff. The circuit judge, appointed by the state assembly, also played a crucial role in local politics by appointing local electoral boards, school trustee electoral boards, and the board of public welfare. With their ability to distribute patronage, courthouse rings played a disproportionate role in Virginia politics.[306]

This linkage of patronage and politics led to the state capitol and the chairman of the State Board of Compensation, who, appointed by the governor, fixed the salaries and expenses of all of the major county officials. Ebbie Combs served as chair-

304 James Sweeney, "Harry Byrd: Vanished Policies and Enduring Principles," *The Virginia Quarterly Review* 52 (Fall: 1976), pp.596-612, Heinemann, pp.33, 123.

305 Wilkinson, pp.16, 69; Clifford Dowdey, "Harry Flood Byrd: Defender of the Faith," *Virginia Record*, January 1956.

306 Key, pp.20-21; for a vivid description of the politics of one courthouse ring see Wilkinson, pp.9-22.

man and acted as the second-most powerful man in the Byrd Organization. After joining forces with Harry Byrd in the 1920s to defeat a highway bond issue, Combs became his main political advisor and a close personal friend. James Latimer, a political writer for the *Richmond Times-Dispatch*, noted that Combs was often referred to as Byrd's "Field Marshall" or more often as "the chief." "Throughout his years in Richmond, Combs was 'the man to see' of things political with Byrd or entree to Byrd. It became almost a ritual for any aspiring young Democrat who wanted to run for office to make a pilgrimage to Richmond to meet Combs and talk things over," he wrote.[307]

Nevertheless, a certain amount of give-and-take existed between the leaders of the Byrd organization and local officials. Candidates for a high office not only had to garner the favor of the high command, but had to test their popularity by touring counties. A common path marked the rise of political leaders in Virginia. In commencing his apprenticeship, the young aspirant generally occupied the position of commonwealth's attorney in a county. He then journeyed to the state Senate after receiving the nod of local organization leaders. If he demonstrated loyalty and gained public exposure he might then serve either as a lieutenant governor or attorney general.[308]

The core of the machine's support and most of its votes lay in rural and Black-Belt Southside Virginia, of which Danville lay at the heart. Governor Almond noted that in the Southside a "consolidation of mores and outlook" existed, meaning that "the vote

---

307 William Bryan Crawley, Jr., *The Governorship of William M. Tuck, 1945-1950: Virginia Politics in the "Golden Age" of the Byrd Organization* (Ph.D. Dissertation, University of Virginia, 1974), p.90; James Latimer, "Virginia Politics," unpublished manuscript, copy in author's possession. For an example of Combs' power, a letter written by Cam Perdue, Commissioner of Revenue to Ben Dillon reads: "Dear sir: Mr. Combs, chairman of the Compensation Board, who sets your salary and mine for our work as Commissioner and Deputy Commissioner of the Revenue, is very much interested in seeing John S. Battle elected our governor. Since Mr. Combs is a good friend of ours I think it would be to our interest to get out every vote we can for Mr. Battle." *Washington Post*, June 10, 1957.

308 Wilkinson, p.24.

is not only large but solidified in support of the organization, and as a result the Southside has exercised a power disproportionate to its part of the over-all population of the state."[309]

The importance of the Southside grew out of an alliance between Black-Belt counties and the Democratic Party in order to maintain white supremacy after reconstruction. V. O. Key theorized that in order to present a solid regional front in national politics on the issue of race, Southern states served as home to one-party rule. In each state the Democratic Party yielded to the desires of Black-Belt whites for maintaining white supremacy in order to maintain political unity. In Black-Belt counties two-party competition could have meant appeals to black voters or the election of black politicians as had happened before the Danville "riot"; therefore, whites worked to ensure the survival of the one-party state in fear that party competition would create a threat to their racial status.[310]

Virginia political leaders, however, claiming to be heirs of an aristocratic tradition, prided themselves in not engaging in the racial demagoguery of a Theodore Bilbo or the flamboyancy of a Huey Long. With a restricted electorate, they simply had no need to do so. Instead they appealed to voters on the basis of creating what they claimed was an efficient and remarkably honest political system run on unchanging principles, an opinion shared by most contemporaries.

Typical of Virginian attitudes, Virginius Dabney, the editor of the *Richmond Times-Dispatch*, observed, "The organization yields immense power, and that power is sometimes abused, but the fact remains that Virginia officialdom has far more integrity than is to be found in many states." He claimed that the machine gave most citizens what they wanted by not moving "faster than public opinion induces or forces it to move."[311]

---

309 Ibid., p. 120.
310 Key, p. 8, 11.
311 For instance see James Sweeney; Virginius Dabney, "What Do We Think of Senator Byrd's Machine," *Saturday Evening Post*, January 7, 1950.

No matter what the general public wanted, however, the initiatives of Harry Byrd and his political allies ultimately reflected the desires and interests of their powerful political supporters. Colgate Darden, who served as governor of Virginia during World War II, observed that "organizations don't reform from within. An organization reflects the power of an individual and his friends... Political machines must maintain their base of power, and, therefore, cannot reform themselves. They either maintain their power structure or are replaced," Darden argued. If Harry Byrd's political inflexibility was a philosophical position it also was one of necessity.[312]

Although the lack of two-party competition kept the organization in power, its dependence upon it meant that its survival rested upon the maintenance of rigid and unchanging social and political structures, symbolized by the poll tax, white supremacy, and low-wage labor. Byrd and other machine leaders saw any social change as dangerous and detrimental to their interests and those of the state. One machine leader liked to think of the Byrd ring "as government by gentlemen." However, in order for gentlemen to rule the deference of those who were not patricians had to be maintained.[313]

The Impact of the New Deal and World War II on Virginia

Virginia's economy experienced massive growth during the 1930s and 1940s. Per capita income in the state rose from $384 to $1,228 between 1930 and 1950. The population of Virginia also grew from 2,421,851 in 1930 to 3,318,680 in 1950 as people outside of the state came to work in the defense industry or the expanding federal bureaucracy in Washington, D.C. New Deal programs and World War II defense spending raised the wages of ordinary Virginians and provided them with new jobs. Instead of

---

312 James Latimer, Interviews with Colgate Whitehead Darden and William Munford Tuck, 1975, Accession #10139, University of Virginia Library, Charlottesville, Va.

313 William Manchester, "The Byrd Machine," *Harpers*, November 1952.

seeing these changes as opportunities, however, Harry Byrd and organization leaders saw them as potential dangers. They found the growth of federal bureaucracy, urbanization, industrialization, and unions detrimental to the interests of the rural elites, which made up the power base of the Byrd machine.[314]

The power of the Byrd machine rested on one-party rule and a restricted electorate, which gave rural Southside elites a disproportionate amount of political power. County elites held a feudal ideology which conceived of each man as having inherited, by nature and family, his own unique role in the social order. The ideal society was one in which the inferior respected authority and remained submissive. They opposed outside intrusions, such as New Deal programs or labor organizers, as agitators who threatened what they saw as Southern values. Many were the champions of white supremacy and the myth of the lost cause.[315]

According to economic historian Gavin Wright, the "economic underpinning" of the Southern elite "was the low-wage labor market, and the implicit coalition included not just planters but lumber and sawmill operators, textile mill owners, and other employers." They united not only on racial issues, but in opposition to federal bureaucracy and social spending. Despite being the poorest region in the country and having Southerners on key congressional committees, the South received the lowest level of per capita federal spending in the nation.[316]

At first Southerners supported President Franklin Roosevelt and the New Deal. Virginia stood as a case in point. The Depression, party loyalty, and Roosevelt's popularity brought Harry Byrd's support for the New Deal's earliest programs. That support soon turned into open animosity, however, as Byrd and other Southern political leaders saw it as a dangerous threat to the South. The

---

314 Thomas Jefferson Center for Political Economy, University of Virginia, *Statistical Abstract of Virginia, Vol. II* (Charlottesville: The Michie Company, 1970), p.10; *Statistical Abstract, Vol. I*, p.5.

315 Numan V. Bartley, *The New South: 1945-1980* (United States: Louisiana State University Press, 1995), pp.32-33;

316 Gavin Wright, *Old South, New South* (United States: Basic Books, 1986), p.259.

New Deal intruded into the rule of local elites by interfering with low-wage labor markets and by threatening more change through political realignment with Northern liberals, blacks, and unionists.[317]

Virginia's senior senator, Carter Glass, and Harry Byrd were among the earliest Southern congressman to oppose the New Deal. Glass claimed that it was "an utterly dangerous effort of the federal government to transplant Hitlerism to every corner of the nation." Like Glass, Byrd became a national figure as he spoke out more and more vigorously against the New Deal and organized labor. He saw them as a threat to Virginia's labor market and social order. Virginia business groups such as the Chamber of Commerce and Manufacturers Association often complained that federal programs were upsetting pay scales.

Relaying their fears, Governor William Tuck wrote Byrd in 1946, "The officials of these federal agencies apparently are utterly indifferent to the disruption they are causing in pay scales of the state government and private industry in Virginia. As an example, Mrs. Hay, Mr. Bradford's secretary, whose salary is $2,160, was recently offered $3,000 by the Veteran's Administration for the same, or perhaps less difficult work," he continued, worried that an increase in pay scales would mean an increase in state expenditures. Byrd responded, "I entirely agree with you and have done my utmost to hold these salaries down. If it had not been for me they would have increased thirty per cent the first of last July instead of fourteen."[318]

The Fair Employment Practices Commission, which threatened to overturn racially based pay scales and hiring, also served as a source of worry for Byrd. He strongly voiced opposition to the bill, calling it "the most dangerous proposal ever seriously considered

317 Ronald Heinemann, *Depression and New Deal in Virginia* (Charlottesville: University Press of Virginia, 1983), p.137; Alan Brinkley, "The South and the New Deal."

318 James Patterson, *Congressional Conservatism and the New Deal* (United States: University of Kentucky Press, 1967), p.13; William Tuck to Harry Byrd, Oct 13, 1946; Harry Byrd to William Tuck, Nov. 6, 1946, Tuck papers, folder 3341:

by Congress during my thirteen years of service in the Senate of the United States." Addressing Congress he warned that by establishing another "inquisitorial bureau of the Federal Government" the FEPC "will take a long step toward a totalitarian government, which in the end, means a Communist state."[319] Complementing his tough stances on labor and civil rights, Byrd was best known as an advocate of balanced budgets and low taxes.

Congressman Howard Smith of Alexandria, Virginia, became much better known as an opponent of organized labor. Convinced that it presented a threat to the American way of life, the labor union movement became an obsession of his. Smith opposed collective bargaining, the Wagner Act, and the NLRB, which he claimed "was thoroughly impregnated with Communists, reds, and pinks of every hue, seeking to place the American working man in a state of peonage to the CIO." In 1938 the Roosevelt administration believed that Smith was so "reactionary" that they placed him on a purge list.[320]

In turn, Harry Byrd opposed a third term for Roosevelt in 1940, maintained a golden silence in the 1944 campaign, and excused himself from the 1948 election by saying that he was too busy with his apple harvest to do anything. Latimer argues that "Byrd probably knew what he was doing politically; most of his conservative, upper-crust, well-to-do Virginia backers in busi-

---

319 Byrd papers, Box 366, Speech January 29, 1946 on the FEPC.
320 Bruce Dierenfield, *Keeper of the Rule: Congressman Howard W. Smith of Virginia* (Charlottesville: University Press of Virginia, 1987), p.84; Smith papers, Box 193, File: Labor Speech in House 1/15/46; James Gross, *The Reshaping of the National Labor Relations Board* (Albany: State University of New York Press, 1981), p.69. Overall Byrd Organization leaders preferred dealing with the AFL than the CIO, which opposed the poll tax and segregation. For example, Combs wrote one local Organization man in Harrisonburg:"E. J. Shave, Secretary of the AFL, Newport News, Virginia, has just been in my office complaining because the AFL organization in Harrisonburg has been refused a hall in which to hold their meetings. Shave says that the CIO is certain to come to Harrisonburg and organize if the AFL gets out. If you have to have either the AFL or the CIO, I would much prefer the AFL...Write Shave and tell him he can have a hall...I am sending a copy of this letter to Senator Byrd at Winchester and I suggest that you communicate with him about this." See Harry Byrd papers, Box 175, Combs to Switzer, Sept. 6, 1941.

ness, banking and industry shared his anti-FDR and anti-Truman feelings."[321] Despite such fierce opposition, Roosevelt remained a popular figure for most Virginians.

Lloyd Robinette, a Roosevelt supporter, recalled "sitting in the Colonial Theater in Richmond" and watching a newsreel. "I saw the president and many of the Republican leaders in Congress on the screen, but there was not a ripple of applause. But when the face of the great humanitarian, Franklin D. Roosevelt, was on the screen applause was spontaneous all over the house showing that this great man is still enshrined in the hearts of the ordinary people of America," he remembered. Robinette's observations were reflected in the way Virginians repeatedly voted for Roosevelt. In 1936 and 1940 he received over 67 percent of the votes in Virginia. In 1944 he received 59 percent of the votes, despite the fact that a Republican ad, linking itself to Harry Byrd and placed in state newspapers the day before the election, claimed that a vote for Roosevelt was like a vote for Earl Browder of the Communist Party.[322]

Supporters of the president formed the core of an anti-organization faction within Virginia's Democratic Party. Leaders of this faction came out of the Byrd organization, but slowly distanced themselves from it as it attacked Roosevelt. The governorship of James Price marked their defining experience.

Price, a liberal who was widely popular with Virginia voters, served as lieutenant governor and announced his desire to run for governor in 1937. Fearing to openly oppose him because of his enormous popularity, and yet leery of his support for the New Deal and electoral reform, the Byrd organization supported him only halfheartedly. Nevertheless, Price went on to win 86.1 percent of the votes in the Democratic primary.[323]

---

321 Latimer, p.27.
322 Martin Hutchinson papers, Box 9, Lloyd Robinette to Hutchinson, January 21, 1947; Ralph Eisenberg, *Virginia Votes, 1924-1968* (Charlottesville, University of Virginia, 1971), pp.101, 117, 137; *Richmond Times-Dispatch* November 9, 1944.
323 Heinemann, p.189; Elizabeth Williams, *The Anti-Byrd Organization Movement in Virginia, 1948-1949* (M.A. thesis, University of Virginia, 1969), p.8.

In Price's first session with the General Assembly he won passage of a legislative program that included increased school funding, social security, and a forty-hour work week for women, with little opposition. But after he removed Ebbie Combs from the State Compensation Board, and replaced him with Martin Hutchison, who was known to be one of Byrd's most resolute opponents, the Byrd organization united in opposition against him. From thereafter, a Byrd-dominated General Assembly voted against almost all of his subsequent proposals. One member of the General Assembly claimed that, afterward, the legislature devoted itself to "naming bridges and bedeviling Jim Price."[324]

Despite its few legislative achievements, the administration of James Price marked the high tide of the anti-Byrd faction. After Price left office no more anti-Byrd candidates would win the governor's office in Byrd's lifetime. With a limited and class-skewed electorate, neither could they build a mass following. What is more, as V. O. Key noted, by allying itself with the leading business and financial interests of Virginia, the Byrd machine "in effect brought into camp most of the people which might furnish opposition." Those who were anti-Byrd leaders were often seen as disgruntled eccentrics, erratic idealists, or worse. Without any patronage powers and very few members in the state government, anti-organization leaders simply could not compete on equal terms.[325]

Nonetheless, pockets of anti-organization strength, mostly in urban and industrial areas, existed in Virginia. The Second Congressional District, home of the industrialized Tidewater, including Norfolk and Portsmouth, tended to vote against Byrd candidates. James Latimer argued that it was "probably the state's most cosmopolitan, atypical district." Alleghany County, which lies in western Virginia and is home to paper mills and other industries, also delivered a large anti-Byrd vote. The Ninth District, however, earned the nickname "The Fightin' Ninth" for being a citadel for

---

324 Heinemann, p.190, Crawley, p.92.
325 Key, pp.27-3j4.

anti-organization votes. A coal mining center, it lay wedged between West Virginia, Kentucky, Tennessee, and North Carolina in
Southwestern Virginia and was the poorest section Virginia.[326]

In the 1945 Democratic gubernatorial primary, these areas
gave the strongest support to the anti-Byrd candidate, Moss
Plunkett of Roanoke. Although urban areas were the sources
of his strength, those urban areas with a large industrial workforce gave him the most votes. Leaders of the organization kept
their eye on these sections of Virginia. Seeing them as the consequences of industrialization, they worried over the ramifications
of social change in Virginia and the growth of industrial cities. They
witnessed Virginia, like much of the country, undergo a complete
transformation in one decade.[327]

The Hampton Roads area, a harbor formed at the end of the
Potomac, Rappahannock, and James rivers, experienced the most
population growth and the state's first war boom as it became
a center of shipbuilding and a place to load and provision military forces during World War II. Northern Virginia also grew as
it became home to men and women working as part of the New
Deal or defense establishments. Not to be outdone, Southwest
Virginia, the location of the Ninth Congressional District, grew
quickly once it became a war manufacturing center. In all, defense
expenditures in the Old Dominion grew from $78 million in 1939
to $413 million in 1942.[328]

Population growth created new pressures on Virginia's infra-
structure. Cities lacked adequate housing, public services, health
care, schools, and transportation. Racial tensions in Richmond became visible in 1943 as buses became overcrowded. Jim Crow
laws demanded that blacks sit in the back of the bus, thereby
creating discord as seats sat unused. Virginius Dabney, the editor
of the *Richmond Times-Dispatch*, suggested doing away with street

---

326 Latimer, p. 13.
327 Ibid.
328 Jonathan James Wolfe, *Virginia in World War II* (Ph.D. Dissertation, University of
      Virginia, 1971), pp. 145-148, 174-176, 190.

car segregation laws, but Governor Darden, who could not ignore the complaints of the public and his political allies throughout the state, did not respond to his proposal. White fears of uppity blacks multiplied and so did innuendo. Paranoia increased so much that the state militia took precautions against rumors that blacks everywhere would revolt on the fourth of July and stab white people throughout the state.[329]

In spite of de jure segregation and overt racism, blacks made real gains during the war as better-paying jobs became open to them and their incomes rose. Luther Jackson headed the Negro Voters League, which slowly and quietly registered a small number of black voters, without any cries of opposition. Black and white veterans returning from World War II, with new aspirations and hopes, also voted in large numbers, for the first time.

Veterans groups lobbied to pass a bill, which would exempt all returning veterans from restrictive voting procedures and the poll tax. According to Governor Darden, Harry Byrd argued that soldiers, being scattered and isolated, could not vote intelligently in state contests while the war lasted. [330] Organization leaders in the General Assembly also opposed any special bills for soldiers. Nevertheless, thanks to an intense lobbying campaign by the American Legion, the state passed measures which created a special fund for payment of the poll tax for veterans. The end result, however, amounted to an increase of only ten thousand voters in the electorate.[331]

As social and economic change marked Virginia in the 1940s, James Latimer observed, "with thousands of new residents brought in during World War II, and with thousands of returning World War II veterans, the Virginia of the late 1940s was not entirely the placid political place it used to be." He was right.

---

329 Ibid., pp.182-184; Nancy Armstrong, *The Study of an Attempt Made in 1943 to Abolish Segregation of the Races on Common Carriers in the State of Virginia* (University of Virginia, 1950).
330 Wolfe, pp.75-78, 131-133.
331 Ibid.

Overall, between 1940 and 1948 the ballots cast for president increased, from 293,881 in 1940 to 387,015 in 1948, an increase of 31.7 percent.[332]

Leaders of the Byrd organization attempted to control the social consequences of industrialization and urbanization. With their source of political strength in the rural areas of Virginia, they tried to provide safeguards against the sudden emergence of an anti-Byrd urban electorate. Led by Governor Darden, attempts to attract small factories to Virginia and keep out any large industrial plants characterized Virginia's economic policy. According to Clifford Dowdey, a Virginia journalist, there existed opposition to heavy industry "by powers who desire no rivalry (especially for pools of labor), and a sentimental opposition supported by gentry who simply disliked an industrialized society."[333]

Darden planned to scatter new factories all along the countryside in order to prevent the growth of population centers. "The small scattered industries are the backbone," Byrd concurred. Looking back after retirement, Darden said, "One of the things you have got to remember in assessing Harry's impact is that he was essentially an agrarian. He never understood, nor did he concern himself too much with understanding, the deep problems of an industrial civilization that was beginning to find its place in Virginia."[334]

Harry Byrd and the CIO

In response to the Byrd organization's opposition to organized labor, the CIO Political Action Committee of Virginia announced the launching of an "energetic" campaign to "unseat Senator Byrd and his sinister anti-Democratic machine from office." In a resolution given to the press it drew parallels between Adolf Hitler and Harry Byrd, claiming that both denied people basic rights "as expounded by such great Americans as George Washington, Thomas

---

332 Eisenberg, p. 35; Latimer, p.27.
333 Dowdey, p.28.
334 Wolfe, p.221; Dowdey, p.30; Sweeney, p.601.

Jefferson, Patrick Henry, and Franklin D. Roosevelt." Through the poll tax, voter fraud, and the denial of collective bargaining, it concluded that "the plot of Senator Byrd to capture and rule Virginia is of the same pattern as Adolf Hitler's plot to destroy all democracies and rule the world."[335]

Unfortunately for Byrd, the anti-organization forces in the Democratic Party mobilized in support of Martin Hutchinson's campaign against him in the 1946 Democratic primary. The campaign marked the first time Byrd ever faced electoral opposition since becoming a senator. Hutchinson's campaign came out of the formation of the Committee for Democracy in Virginia, created by loosely organized liberal Democrats in order to oppose the Byrd machine, support the New Deal, increase spending on public services, and reform Virginia by eliminating the poll tax. Led by Martin Hutchinson and Francis Pickens Miller, the committee was not a large organization. Like generals without an army, it functioned mainly to chart strategy.[336]

State Senator Lloyd Robinette saw the Committee for Democracy as the last chance to save Virginia. "Unless something is done and soon the Democratic Party will be destroyed in Virginia. Already its membership is composed of men and women who are even more reactionary than Robert Taft...You have no conception of the situation existing in the Senate of Virginia today. There is hardly a whisper of liberalism in the whole membership, because they are bound to the chariot wheels of Senator Byrd and his crowd of buccaneers." Robinette and others in the anti-machine faction desired to work within the Democratic Party to liberalize it. They believed that if they failed to realign it with the New Deal it would eventually collapse and the Republicans would take over the state.[337]

---

335 *Richmond Times-Dispatch*, January 28, 1946.
336 Ebbie Combs to Byrd, February 6, 1946, Harry Byrd papers, Box 85; Elizabeth Williams, *The Anti-Byrd Organization Movement in Virginia, 1948-1949* (M.A. Thesis, University of Virginia, 1969), p.10; See Hutchinson papers for correspondence regarding the Committee for Democracy in Virginia.
337 Lloyd Robinette to E. H. McConnell, February 18, 1946, Hutchinson papers, Box 7.

Robinette worried that "certain elements in Virginia" would try to "infiltrate" the liberal organization. "We should watch this carefully. We can choose with care our membership on the committees of our organization" and get only "real men and women in each county to join us." Robinette's remarks reveal the uneasy situation anti-Byrd forces found themselves in with relationship to the CIO and organized labor. On one hand, they needed labor, but on the other they believed that they had to keep their distance from it. This dilemma became more and more apparent as Hutchinson's campaign evolved.[338]

Since Hutchinson lacked any real campaign staff or organization of his own, local labor organizers proved to be an integral part of his campaign. Moss Plunkett informed him that unionists and black organizations throughout Virginia were launching a campaign to urge people to pay poll taxes. Some union locals set up separate funds to provide block payments. "In Suffolk area 286 Negroes qualified to vote in ten days, and the work is well underway. In the Roanoke area and in the Lynchburg area and in the Danville area similar work is being done," Plunkett wrote.[339]

The Byrd camp was privy to these activities. We must not forget "the importance of keeping in close touch with developments in Roanoke, Danville, Richmond, Norfolk, Norfolk County, and in certain other counties in the state where there is a possibility of qualifying a large organized labor vote," worried Combs. Byrd fretted over this possibility so much that he was willing to write off urban areas. "I think it important that we do all we can see so that the conservative element pay their poll tax. This can only be done safely I think in the rural communities," he informed Combs.[340]

The primary race proved to be unusual for Virginia. Unlike most political races in Virginia, which had been quiet affairs, Harry

---

338 Ibid.
339 Moss Plunkett to Hutchinson, April 22, 1946, Hutchinson papers, Box 7; *Richmond Times-Dispatch,* July 7, 1946.
340 Combs to Harry Byrd, March 23, 1946 and Byrd to Combs April 4, 1946, Harry Byrd papers, Box 85.

Byrd launched a public campaign against his opponent, hyperbolically linking him to the CIO's political action committee. As Governor Tuck wrote Byrd, "As long as we can keep the CIO fighting you out in the open, I think you are all right." Byrd addressed Virginians on the radio and warned them that "for the first time since Carpet Bagger days, sinister outside influences are seeking to control an election in Virginia...If this effort of foreign labor leaders to defeat me is crushed down by a decisive majority, a setback will be given to the national campaign of the CIO-PAC to dominate our government."[341]

Throughout the campaign, Byrd hit on this theme of labeling his opponent as a CIO-PAC agent. He asserted that the survival of Virginia lay on the table in the coming election. If he were to lose, "we may wake up some morning and find that the dictatorship of labor leaders has been so firmly established that the people will be a long time in recovering control of their government." His campaign staff, in an effort to further frighten Virginia voters, spread a rumor that the CIO-PAC donated one million dollars to Hutchinson's campaign.[342]

Virtually every newspaper in Virginia picked up on Byrd's charges. Thomas Lomax Hunter, a columnist for the *Richmond Times-Dispatch*, declared that the election would determine "whether Virginia wants to remain Virginia or go CIO-PAC." The *Roanoke World-News* stated that the "embarrassing support" given to Hutchinson by the CIO-PAC will arouse Virginia's voters to defeat him. Instead of a race between Hutchinson and Byrd, supporters of the incumbent tried to make it appear to be a race between Byrd and the "foreign" forces of the CIO.[343]

---

341 William Tuck to Byrd, May 15, 1946, Tuck personal papers, file 3262; seventh campaign radio speech, July 29, 1946, Harry Byrd papers, Box 367.

342 Second campaign speech, June 24, 1946, third campaign speech, July 1, 1946, Harry Byrd papers, Box 367.

343 *Richmond Times-Dispatch*, May 12, 1946; for a digest of editorial opinion throughout the state see *Richmond Times-Dispatch*, August 4, 1946.

Despite the statements of Byrd and the newspapers, organized labor supported Hutchinson only indirectly by encouraging people to pay the poll tax and vote. The CIO-PAC did not give any money to Hutchinson. In reality his campaign was starved for funds. He needed money so badly that he could not afford to spend much time away from his law practice to campaign, using his personal earnings as funds for the election.[344]

Labor activists in Virginia also purposely kept the CIO away from his campaign. Clarence Mague, a unionist and civic leader who served as Hutchinson's campaign manager in Norfolk County, wrote the candidate, "I would rather the incumbent not know that I'm a member of any labor organization... I'm sorry to see the CIO bringing in outsiders, because it does more harm than good... I'm afraid the CIO doesn't know much about Virginia politics." A member of the Brotherhood of Locomotive Engineers also warned, "Labor should be very careful in the activities toward your campaign as labor will be watched very close."[345]

Lloyd Robinette argued that Byrd's smear tactics served as evidence that he was "somewhat doubtful of the future." He wrote Hutchinson, "Byrd has played his hand well in this emergency. He has never favored the laboring man, but in this crisis our people have been enraged by these strikes." Another supporter wrote, "He knows there are but a few CIO in Virginia, none in my county as far as I know. He knows that people are tired of strikes and dislocations brought about by strikes and he has hit upon a popular cord with many people."[346] According to Moss Plunkett, "Senator Byrd saw one way out of the disgraceful position he and his political machine were in: to stir up the prejudices of the people of Virginia against labor in general and the CIO in particular."[347]

---

344 Hutchinson campaign ledger, Hutchinson papers, Box 9.
345 Clarence Mague to Hutchinson, June 15, 1946, and G. I. Grasty to Hutchinson, April 28, 1946, Hutchinson papers, Boxes 7, 8.
346 Lloyd Robinette to Hutchinson, May 25, 1946 and Floyd Robinette to Hutchinson, June 26, 1946, Moss Plunkett to Hutchinson, August 8, 1946, Hutchinson papers, Boxes 7, 8, 9.
347

Byrd was not the only organization candidate to use the CIO as a whipping boy in his campaign. Howard Smith faced opposition for his congressional seat as well. Like Byrd, he charged that his opponent, a mild-mannered lady, represented part of a plot by the CIO to defeat him and other conservative congressmen. "This new swarm of carpetbaggers who are invading the Southern states to take over the political affairs are impregnated and indoctrinated with communism," Smith claimed. "The swarm of minor hirelings who propose to do the actual field work are but the puppets of a foreign born and foreign conceived plot to spread the fearsome specter of communism over the face of the globe." By boxing their opponents into a corner and launching attack after attack, Byrd and Smith mobilized their constituency to come to their defense.[348]

Martin Hutchinson had little chance of winning, and he knew it. As he told one supporter, "When I entered the campaign I knew I would be up against a well financed political machine and, frankly, it would have been little short of a miracle had I won the nomination." Despite the obstacles his campaign faced, he made an impressive showing at the polls, garnering 35.5 percent of the vote.[349]

Although Howard Smith won even more handily then Byrd, defeating his opponent in the primary by 17,457 to 5,005 votes, Hutchinson and other anti-Byrd leaders looked at the overall results with optimism. "I believe the campaign has shown to Virginia people the fact that the political machine, can, with proper organization, be overthrown in Virginia," Hutchinson wrote. With hope for the future, one of his supporters claimed that his campaign demonstrated that "the Byrd organization has by no means got a unanimous following in Virginia."[350]

---

348 *Congressional Record*, V. 92, April 30, 1946, p.4257.

349 Hutchinson to L. L. Bean, September 12, 1946, Hutchinson papers, Box 9. Ralph Eisenberg, *Virginia Votes, 1924-1968* (Charlottesville, VA: University of Virginia, 1971), p.160.

350 *Richmond Times-Dispatch* August 7, 1946; Hutchinson to W.S. McGraw, August 12, 1946 and W.S McGraw to Hutchinson August 10, 1946, Hutchinson papers, Box 9.

Supporters of Harry Byrd celebrated the election results. Thomas Lomax Hunter wrote, "PAC (Pestilent Alien
Carpetbaggers) proved a dud in Virginia. They didn't get to first
base. Their propaganda fooled some Negroes into voting against
the only white people in the state who can do anything for them."
Leaders of the Byrd organization, nonetheless, remained uneasy.[351]

Just as anti-machine forces saw hope for the future in the
election, Senator Byrd and his allies saw potential danger. Howard
Smith warned Governor Tuck, "We would be feeling right badly
if it were not for the good old conservative country vote. The
way the minority groups combined in the cities throughout the
state seems to be a matter for grave reflection." Smith's analysis
was correct. Hutchinson won majorities in Alexandria, Newport
News, Norfolk, Portsmouth, Radford, and Hopewell, all areas of
military, industrial, or federal employment. More alarming, however, for Byrd leaders, were the activities of labor unions. With a
voter registration drive, the CIO increased the size of the state's
electorate, creating a record turnout in many cities. For example,
in Norfolk 5,000 new voters registered and in Roanoke 1,500
people voted for the first time.[352]

Robert Meade, in a survey of voting activity conducted for
the *Richmond Times-Dispatch* during the election, declared that
Virginia was awakening politically. Despite his documentation of
widespread apathy and low voting turnouts, Meade discovered
that in some areas of Virginia, thanks to labor unions, a new interest in voting could be found. In Lynchburg, for instance, he found
that unions "are now registering new voters at the rate of about
thirty to forty per month." As another example of the changes
taking place, he noted that some saw Danville as a "harbinger of
things to come."[353]

351 *Richmond Times-Dispatch,* August 10, 1946
352 Howard Smith to Tuck, August 9, 1946, Tuck personal papers, file 3267; *Richmond
    Times-Dispatch,* July 7, 1946.
353 *Richmond Times-Dispatch,* May 12 and August 4, 1946.

The number of voters in Danville, which lay in the middle of the Southside, doubled between 1944 and 1946 thanks to the CIO. During World War II, it had successfully organized the workers of Dan River Mills textile company. With over 12,000 members, the union became the largest CIO local in Virginia. By 1946, 8,700 registered voters could be counted in Danville. In June, the new voters swept the local Byrd linked Good Government Club out of the city government. A similar movement in Norfolk put a "people's ticket" on the city council. Although the political movements in Norfolk and Danville succeeded in influencing local politics, neither had an effect on local Democratic Parties, which continued to nominate Byrd candidates for the state assembly and Congress, and remained in the control of local elites.[354]

In spite of winning the Democratic primary, Byrd continued to concern himself with these voting trends and display deep anxiety. Up to the regular November election he pondered over the possibility that the CIO might throw its weight behind the Republicans or with one of the two independent candidates. "I have definite information from a reliable source that the Political Action Committee of the CIO is quietly organizing to scratch me next Tuesday. I expected this to occur and do not know to what extent it will actually occur, but I think we should be prepared for it." Despite his fears, he won the election soundly with over 64 percent of the total votes.[355]

Although organized labor played decisive roles in some counties in Virginia, one must not overemphasize its strength throughout the whole state. Hutchinson received 81,605 votes, of which only fraction could be traced to the work of the CIO-PAC. It is unclear exactly how many members the CIO in fact had in Virginia. V. O. Key estimated that it had forty thousand members and no more than ten thousand voters. The actual number was probably a little higher. But in any case, organized labor could not

---

354 *Danville Register,* June 9-11, 1948
355 Harry Byrd to Ebbie Combs, October 30, 1946, Combs papers, Box 1; Eisenberg, p. 152.

have contributed more than a quarter of his votes, even with a high estimate. Nevertheless, any addition of new voters became magnified in Virginia's small electorate and troubled the leaders of the Byrd Organization who saw any opposition as worrisome. As Lloyd Robinette observed, "I find that the big boys are still fearful. They don't know what is being done. They think that there is some sort of secret organization in Virginia which is being augmented daily, and which may be a deciding factor in Virginia someday." The structure of its power base made the existence of any alternative dangerous to the Byrd machine.[356]

More important than its numbers, it was what labor unions represented to the Byrd machine that really mattered to them. The organization's power rested precariously on a restricted electorate and a one-party political system dependent upon Southside, Virginia. A well-organized anti-organization force could undermine Virginia's political oligarchy by creating a new coalition inside of the Republican Party or, more likely, by splitting the state's Democratic Party. Senator Byrd's attacks against organized labor helped to forestall any such possibility by marginalizing any opposition to the Byrd machine as foreign, dangerous, and upsetting to the state's social and racial order.

During the 1960s the Byrd machine would see the civil rights movement as an even greater threat to its power, opposing it even more tenaciously. At one point it shut down the public school system in a feeble attempt to stop integration. It had great reason to do so. Once the civil rights movement pressured Congress into passing the civil rights Act of 1964, which eliminated the poll tax, the power of the Byrd machine collapsed.

The source of the machine's power went back to the turn of the century with the establishment of the poll tax and legal racial segregation following the defeat of the Readjuster coalition after the Danville "riot." From that period until the 1960s politics

---

356 V. O. Key, *Southern Politics in State and Nation* (Knoxville: The University of Tennessee Press, 1996), p.32; Lloyd Robinette to Hutchinson, January 1, 1947, Hutchinson papers, Box 9.

in Virginia, and the South, were dominated by a small group of elites who supported the Democratic Party, white supremacy, and states' rights, and sought to limit the power of the federal government. Their economic power rested on maintaining a segregated, nonunion, and low-wage labor market separate and distinct from the rest of the country.

The major events in the history of Danville, Virginia, from being the last capital of the Confederacy when Jefferson Davis fled Richmond; the success of the Readjuster coalition in Danville and their overthrow by local Democrats; the importance of white supremacy in the city, typified by the murder of John Moffett; to the 1939 strike at Dan River Mills and the success of the TWUA in the 1940s are all a part of this larger history of the South. On one hand they show how elites tried to maintain their power and on the other they show how not only they, but also all classes of people, aspired and worked to create a better future for themselves and their region—a future that we know today.

A NOTE ON THE AUTHOR

Michael Swanson received his master's degree in history from the University of Virginia in 1998. He is a professional writer and trader and serves as the head editor of WallStreetWindow. com where he writes about global investment trends. For updates and more information on the history of the American South and Danville, Virginia go to his website DanvilleVirginiaHistory.com.

CPSIA information can be obtained at www.ICGtesting.com
Printed in the USA
LVOW132008050912

297533LV00022B/67/P